A Description and History of the Pianoforte

Also from Westphalia Press
westphaliapress.org

The Idea of the Digital University

Dialogue in the Roman-Greco World

The Politics of Impeachment

International or Local Ownership?: Security Sector Development in Post-Independent Kosovo

Policy Perspectives from Promising New Scholars in Complexity

The Role of Theory in Policy Analysis

ABC of Criminology

Non-Profit Organizations and Disaster

The Idea of Neoliberalism: The Emperor Has Threadbare Contemporary Clothes

Donald J. Trump's Presidency: International Perspectives

Ukraine vs. Russia: Revolution, Democracy and War: Selected Articles and Blogs, 2010-2016

Iran: Who Is Really In Charge?

Stamped: An Anti-Travel Novel

A Strategy for Implementing the Reconciliation Process

Issues in Maritime Cyber Security

A Different Dimension: Reflections on the History of Transpersonal Thought

Contracting, Logistics, Reverse Logistics: The Project, Program and Portfolio Approach

Unworkable Conservatism: Small Government, Freemarkets, and Impracticality

Springfield: The Novel

Lariats and Lassos

Ongoing Issues in Georgian Policy and Public Administration

Growing Inequality: Bridging Complex Systems, Population Health and Health Disparities

Designing, Adapting, Strategizing in Online Education

Secrets & Lies in the United Kingdom: Analysis of Political Corruption

Pacific Hurtgen: The American Army in Northern Luzon, 1945

Natural Gas as an Instrument of Russian State Power

New Frontiers in Criminology

Feeding the Global South

Beijing Express: How to Understand New China

Demand the Impossible: Essays in History as Activism

A Description and History of the Pianoforte and of the Older Keyboard Stringed Instruments

by A. J. Hipkins

Wood Engravings by John Hipkins

WESTPHALIA PRESS
An imprint of Policy Studies Organization

A Description and History of the Pianoforte and of the Older Keyboard Stringed Instruments

All Rights Reserved © 2018 by Policy Studies Organization

Westphalia Press
An imprint of Policy Studies Organization
1527 New Hampshire Ave., NW
Washington, D.C. 20036
info@ipsonet.org

ISBN-13: 978-1-63391-716-3
ISBN-10: 1-63391-716-9

Cover design by Jeffrey Barnes:
jbarnesbook.design

Daniel Gutierrez-Sandoval, Executive Director
PSO and Westphalia Press

Updated material and comments on this edition
can be found at the Westphalia Press website:
www.westphaliapress.org

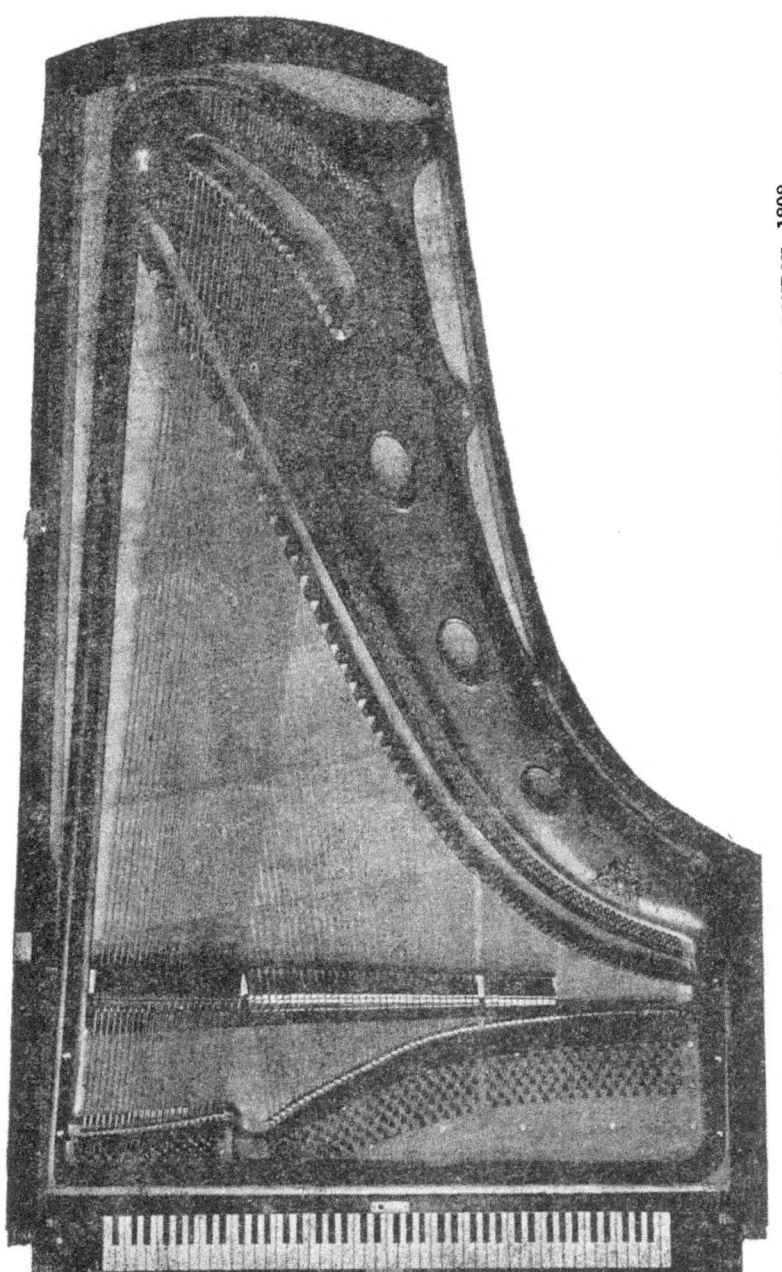

STEEL FRAME CONCERT GRAND PIANOFORTE BY JOHN BROADWOOD AND SONS, LONDON, 1898.

[The Right of Translation is Reserved.]

NOVELLO'S
MUSIC PRIMERS AND EDUCATIONAL SERIES.

A DESCRIPTION AND HISTORY

OF THE

PIANOFORTE

AND

OF THE OLDER KEYBOARD STRINGED INSTRUMENTS

BY

A. J. HIPKINS, F.S.A.

AUTHOR OF THE ARTICLES ON THE PIANOFORTE IN THE "DICTIONARY OF MUSIC AND MUSICIANS" AND IN THE "ENCYCLOPÆDIA BRITANNICA," ALSO OF "MUSICAL INSTRUMENTS, HISTORIC, RARE AND UNIQUE."

THE WOOD ENGRAVINGS BY JOHN HIPKINS.

PRICE TWO SHILLINGS AND SIXPENCE.
In paper boards, Three Shillings.

LONDON: NOVELLO AND COMPANY, LIMITED.
NEW YORK: THE H. W. GRAY CO., SOLE AGENTS FOR THE U.S.A.

Part 1.

THE PIANOFORTE.

Since the Introduction of Iron into the Construction.
From 1820.

There is no musical instrument so extensively used as the pianoforte, and there is certainly none so little understood by the player, in the construction, or the legitimate treatment according to the construction. It would be more intimately known if the performer had to tune it, but the difficulty of tuning renders the employment of a specialist in that art necessary. Few piano players know more about a piano than that the sounds are caused by hammers striking against wire strings. There has, however, arisen in our leading music schools a desire to know more, and students are not now satisfied to remain unacquainted with the nature of their instrument. To assist those who are curious about its construction is one of the objects for which this book is written.

I have chosen to start from the introduction of iron in the construction of the pianoforte, about 1820, as convenient for my purpose, regarding the entirely wooden framed piano as appertaining to an historical division, in which the precursors of the piano, the clavichord, virginal or spinet, and harpsichord will be found.

All pianofortes, without distinction as to period, country of production, or maker, have in common and from necessity certain structural features, liable it may be to variation, but always proper to the instrument. These constructive details are independent of the form of the instrument, or its position; whether it is laid down horizontally as in a grand or square piano, or is stood up vertically as in an upright. But in no instance can one of them be absent. Looking at a pianoforte it is to be regarded as a chest or box, partly external case and partly framing, but neither separable from the other; the case and under frame of wood and the upper frame of iron or steel being adapted and combined to withstand the strain of the strings tightly stretched above ; this composite structure forming the instrument proper, and upon which, in the first place the individual or characteristic tone of the instrument depends.

The wrest-plank or tuning-pin block holds the tuning, or wrest-pins. It is required to be of great solidity, on account of the absolute rigidity demanded by the enormous strain of the strings. There is some loss of strength unavoidable from the boring of the holes in which the pins are inserted, but this is restored when the pins are driven in, and the wrest-plank is even stiffened, as the pins are rather larger than the holes. They are made with a fine thread to render their movement under the tuning-hammer smooth.

In regarding a pianoforte according to its factors in construction, the strings have the first place, due to the fact that it is by their vibrations we are made sensible of the tone, and of its special quality as pianoforte tone. They are attached to the wrest-pins by a coil twisted round each pin, the near end of the string being passed through a small hole bored through the substance of the iron pin. At their farther ends the strings are looped upon pins fixed to the metal string-plate that goes round the inner curved side to the end of the case. The strings are of cast steel wire in batches of increasing diameter from the treble downwards, in the bass of the instrument overspun with a finer copper or mixed metal wire to make the rate of vibration slower. The sound to be obtained from the strings, owing to their slender diameter and restricted contact with the air, is so weak that a resonance factor or sound-board is indispensable to reinforce their feeble tone and make it satisfactory to the ear. The technical name of this board is the belly. There are two hardwood bridges glued upon the belly, or, in some instances a continuous bridge, the function of which is to transmit the vibrations of the strings to the belly, and reproduce them in vibrations of the fibrous substance of the wood ; thereby adequately increasing the sound.

The instrument so far constructed is now complete, case, framing, strings, bridges, and belly, and musical sound can be produced from the strings by twanging or striking them ; but a mechanical apparatus is still required to make the instrument a pianoforte, so that by keys, intermediate mechanism, and hammers, there shall be response to the player's touch. By such an apparatus the interesting and beautiful varieties of his art are evoked. Combining with it the dampers, to stop sound when not required, we have now the complete action. Not exactly essential, yet so necessary in modern music as not to be left out, are the pedal movements, by which, with the right foot always, and the left foot when the action can be shifted away from one of the strings of each note, the player controls very beautiful acoustic effects.

A grand or square piano, when the cover or top is raised, shows much of the inner structure, the strings with their wrest-pins, the wrest-plank, metal framing, and the belly. Also parts of the action, as the hammers and dampers; and the keyboard with its ivory and ebony notes when the front of the instrument is opened. An upright piano shows less of the structure but more of the action. The ribbing of the back of the belly by the belly-bars, and the wooden beams or bracings which form the under structure, can only be seen from beneath a grand piano, or from behind an upright one, when the usual screen of canvas is unscrewed and removed. In a square piano they are invisible owing to a thick wooden bottom which here forms an essential part of the structure.

The remarkable difference there is between the modern and the old pianos is due to the immense improvement which has taken place in the drawing of music wire, increasing its tenacity to a high degree. Step by step the piano has advanced with this improvement; adding strength of structure, as it has been possible to employ strings of greater diameter, weight, and tension; changing iron for wood where necessary for resistance, and admitting larger hammers, with a vastly increased possibility of blow to impel them to the strings; also by improving the action, so as to increase the range of the hammer's velocity and place it more directly under the player's control. The modern virtuoso owes his crashing chords, in the first place, to the successful experimenters in cast steel wire.

The strings, as already said, are the vibrators, initiating the distinctive quality of tone of the instrument, but amenable in this respect to the relative elasticity of the wood and iron, of which the framing, which resists the draught or tension of the strings, is constructed; and also to the peculiar strain or stress along certain angles, inevitable from the harp-like shape of the instrument and its scale of stringing, the shortest strings being in the treble and the longest in the bass. The strings not only vibrate as a whole between the points of bearing on the wrest-plank and sound-board bridge, but in sections of diminishing length, which combine the octave, twelfth, super-octave, and so on, to an indefinitely high number, with the fundamental tone we hear and recognise as a particular note. These harmonic divisions of the strings are now known as the partial tones, above the lowest or fundamental as the upper partial tones. Their existence in the shorter sections adds to the brilliant character of the note; if we could hear the fundamental partial alone it would be dull indeed. It is important that the complex nature of a musical note should be understood; we never hear a fundamental tone alone; we never hear an upper partial tone without some mixture of shorter vibrating sections, unless it is by the employment of resonators which are contrived to exclude those auxiliary tones so that we may hear the simple note without them. It requires an effort of the imagination to mentally conceive a piano string when vibrating, the molecules of which it is composed alternately expanding and contracting owing to the agitation caused by the hammer blow. The first impulse excites their vibration to the bridges, but in the return, owing to a natural law, it is arrested at points about the half, the third, fourth, fifth, sixth, seventh, &c., of the string until renewed by the elasticity of the wire regaining its potentiality. These points of rest are called nodes; they are really points of latent energy and opposing force, and are never absolutely quiescent. The vibrating sections are known as loops. We have to realise that while the whole length of string vibrates, that two halves, three thirds, four fourths, &c., are vibrating simultaneously or coming to a state of apparent rest in nodes, and finally to absolute rest and silence as the energy imparted to them by the blow expires. The loops make their excursion from the direct line, the vibrations being transverse or across the direction of the string's length. The harmonics or sectional notes, carrying their own shorter sections or partials, may be brought out by gently touching the strings forming a note upon the corresponding node to the harmonic desired, so that at one half when vibration is incited by the hammer we hear the octave, the string now divided in two sections; at one third we hear the twelfth, now divided in three sections, and so on. In a good pianoforte it is possible to hear the series of these harmonics as far as the tenth, and, with some uncertainty, even higher partials may be perceived. The order of the partial tones forming a fundamental note and its harmonics is thus shown:—

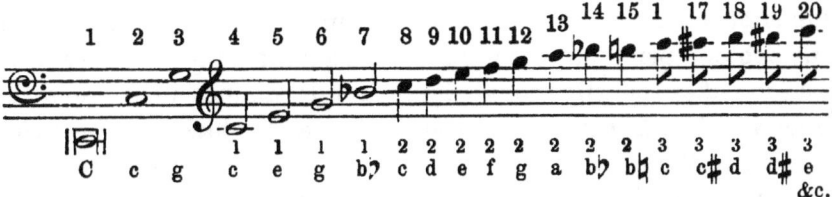

I have indicated the different octaves by the time value of the notes, but the width of the musical interval is in the ascending order always diminishing. The seventh and fourteenth, it should be observed, are flatter in pitch than the corresponding notes we use; the eleventh is sharper than f^2, and the thirteenth is flatter than a^2; the deviations from consonance being more frequent as the intervals become smaller.

Helmholtz* attributes differences in qualities of tone, such as between a piano and a harmonium, a clarinet and a flute or an oboe, to differences in the relative force or preponderance of these partial tones. As already indicated, the full-sounding harmonious intervals are those of longer section between the first and eighth, and that as we ascend the harmonic scale dissonance becomes more and more frequent, until, as may be heard with an Æolian harp when the wind is strong, it becomes excruciating.

The greater elasticity of iron as compared with wood does not allow the lesser vibrating sections or upper partial tones of a string to die away as soon as they would with the less elastic wood.† The consequence is that in instruments where iron or steel preponderates in the framing there is a longer *sostenente* or singing tone, and increasingly so as there is a higher tension or strain on the wire. Where wood preponderates these vibrating sections die out sooner. The extremes of these conditions are a metallic whizzing or tinkling, and a dull "woody" tone. The middle way, as so often happens,

---

* Helmholtz, "On the Sensations of Tone as a physiological basis for the Theory of Music," translated by A. J. Ellis. Second English edition, Longmans, 1885, pp. 18-25. See also Koenig, "Quelques Expériences d'Acoustique." Paris, 1882, pp. 235-6.

† Sir George Grove's "Dictionary of Music and Musicians," Vol. IV., Art. "Tone' (A. J. H.), p. 142. Macmillan, London, 1889.

is to be preferred. The vibrations of a string are periodic, in more or less rapid pulsations according to the pitch, increasing as the pitch becomes more acute, slackening as it becomes lower. In the fundamental note the vibrations are simply pendular—that is, like the bob of a pendulum; every sectional addition, the octave, twelfth, &c., modifies the vibrational figure and determines a change in the note which the ear readily appreciates, and which can be made evident to the eye. To continue this inquiry would be to travel too far into acoustics; some difficulties may, however, be removed that interfere with the conception of compound vibration if we try to realise that the disturbance in the string is molecular; the harmonic sections vibrating in countless atoms instead of in the swing of a solid substance which the string appears to be when it is at rest, and in several or many different ways at the same period of time; on which fact, as Lord Rayleigh has said, depends the possibility of music.

Another consideration affecting quality of tone is the blow of the hammer against the strings. The "striking place" or point of contact of the hammer has to be considered, as well as the material of the hammer and its surface, and the degree of force or velocity of the blow. Also the directness with which the blow is delivered to ensure the strings forming a note, usually three in number, being agitated equally; good and satisfactory tone being impossible without this care as to measured incidence and directness of the blow. The line of the striking place, in agreement with that of the hammers, is required to be a straight one. In due relation to the player's touch the hammers strike the strings with a gradation of velocities, the zero of which is the faintest *pianissimo* obtainable by the finger; from which we ascend to the strongest *fortissimo* the most muscular pianist can produce. Of course much depends upon the mechanical apparatus through which the momentum given by the pianist is transmitted; its value as a machine, and the order it is in, as well as the quality and elasticity of the hammer. But with the best contrived action, in the best working order, it needs no special gift of perception to comprehend the importance of the impetus given by the player to the key; the measured accuracy of attack, and, of no less importance, the *personal* quality of the touch, which, in some pianists, may be classed as a gift, analogous, in this respect, to a singer's voice. Touch is as varied as all other attributes pertaining to, and distinguishing, individuals. Education may improve, but it cannot create. The personal character of touch is as different among players as we are told thumb-prints differ.

The surface quality of the felt of which the hammer is formed has to be taken into account, as well as the hammer's elasticity, in affecting the length of contact of the hammer with the strings, and consequently the quality of tone. Even in this small interval of time the contact affects the continuance or extinction of the high upper partial tones or short vibrating sections of the string on which very often the incisiveness of the tone-quality depends. When we think of the rapidity with which a string goes through its various phases of vibration, the whole being accomplished, at middle C, in about 259 to 270 pulsations in a second, according to the pitch chosen, or, at treble clef C, 518 to 540, we can understand the difference the damping power belonging to the hammer can make, according to its surface texture modifying the contact with the strings.

As already said, the due complement to a vibrator is a reinforcer or resonator, and this exists in the pianoforte in the belly or sound-board. The mutual action of a vibrator and a resonator depends very much upon their relative energy. If this is near an equilibrium the one will modify the other, but if there is a great disproportion, then the weaker of these factors is taken captive and becomes more or less effaced. The belly of a piano is free to the surrounding air, and although, as nearly all wood, and especially fir wood, it has a note proper to itself, the enormous controlling energy of the strings overcomes that note and its vibrations are absorbed. It is to the broad vibrating surface of the belly, in contact with the air, we owe the reinforcement which increases the tone of the instrument so as to make it satisfactorily audible. Thus considered, the strings, within the conditions stated of framing and incitement by blow, may be regarded as vibrators, and as directly responsible for the tone-quality of the pianoforte; while the belly is responsible for the due presentation and reinforcement of the characteristic tone of the instrument, as initiated by the hammer from the touch of the player. If the belly is defective it will absorb or damp the tone it should transmit. A visual analogue is a looking-glass; a good plate effectively silvered will reflect what is before it perfectly, a bad plate imperfectly, and when concave to distortion. But it cannot add to the objects it reflects, or alter their relative positions.

We have now arrived at understanding that the quality of tone of a piano, of whatever form or model, depends, in the first place, upon the strings, the case, and framing structure; and in the next, upon the hammers and mechanical action manipulated by the player; and lastly, upon resonance to increase the quantity and duration of the tone, due to the belly in response to the mechanical impulse of the strings, given in multitudinous small blows through the belly-bridge. To explain and extend these fundamental conceptions we will consider separately the strings, the wrest-plank, the case structure, including the wood and iron framing, the belly and bridges completing the instrument as such, and, finally, the mechanical action, which includes the hammers the keyboard, and the pedals.

THE STRINGS.

Wire-drawing and stringed instruments with keyboards seem to have appeared together in Europe somewhere about the middle of the fourteenth century. The earliest wire-drawing mill is said to have been erected then at Nuremberg. Iron wire was first drawn, the ore after selection being treated with charcoal fuel. The wire used in the last century, whether iron or brass, was of feeble tenacity, and up to the middle of the present century it was easy to break the treble strings and force a piano out of tune. The gradual improvement in piano wire has not been confined to one place or country. Early in this century Nuremberg wire was in use, but about 1820 it had to give way to Berlin wire. In 1834 a great stride was made by Webster of Birmingham, who brought out a steel wire to replace the iron wire, the tensile properties of which it much exceeded. It is true that steel wire had been tried in Germany, but presumably with little success, as iron wire, previous to Webster's improvement, prevailed everywhere. In 1850 Müller, of Vienna, took the lead. In 1854 Webster and Horsfall, of Birmingham, introduced an invention, attributed to Horsfall, of a tempered cast steel music wire of great value; but the preference has again reverted to Germany, the wire of Pöhlmann, of Nuremberg, being the most in favour at the present time with the leading pianoforte makers.* The official testings at the Chicago Exhibition, in August, 1893, with Riehle Brothers' machine,† give Pöhlmann the first place for tenacity or breaking weight. The breaking point of his wire being for No. 13 (diameter 0·030 English inch, Brown & Sharpe's micrometer gauge), 325 lb.; No. 14 (0·031), 335 lb.; No. 15 (0·034), 350 lb.; No. 16 (0·035), 400 lb.; and No. 17 (0·037), 415 lb. The gauge No. 16, diameter, inch ·035, being equivalent to the Birmingham gauge No. 20. The Imperial Standard Wire Gauge, sanctioned by the Board of Trade in 1884, does not yet appear to have come into general use, although the old gauges are not uniform as measures of diameter.

The above testings are sufficient to justify the opinion of Dr. William Pole, F.R.S., that cast steel wire combines greater strength and elasticity than any other material known to us. Notwithstanding the toughness of its texture it is easily wound round the wrest-pins. Its elasticity is demonstrated by the length of time well-made pianos now remain in tune, even against formidable use. As I have already said, the modern pianoforte only became possible by the great improvement of music wire.

The gradations in diameter of the wire used in pianos is numbered on the Birmingham gauge from about 13 to 24. Beyond the last diameter we approach the liability to the inharmonious proper tones characteristic of the steel bar. Some of these proper tones are not aliquot and may be very dissonant.

The least diameter of piano strings is coincident with the shortest length; that is to say, in the highest notes. The increase of diameter in pianoforte scaling is determined by experience, and is a compromise attributable to the necessary contraction of the scale in order to bring the dimensions of the instrument within reasonable limits. It is usual to regard the treble clef, c^2 of the tuning fork, as one foot length between the bridges, although it may in practice exceed that measurement. By the canon of length of vibrating strings, the octave below—that is, middle c^1 of the same diameter and tension—should be approximately two feet long; bass clef c, four feet; C below the bass clef,

---

* "Dictionary of Music and Musicians"—"String" (A. J. H.), Vol. III., pp. 744-5; and Bucknall Smith, "Wire, its manufacture and uses" (London and New York, 1892), pp. 19-23.

† "Zeitschrift für Instrumentenbau" (Leipzig, 1894), p. 300.

eight; and the lowest C of all, sixteen feet. The normal scaling, however, ends at or near the bass clef f; the reduced length of the lower notes being made up for by increased diameter and consequent weight. In the last octave the strings are overspun with fine copper or white metal wire to increase their weight sufficiently to make up for the disproportionate vibrating lengths. The "overstrung" or cross-strung bass admits of longer bass strings. The third canon of the string, length and thickness being the first and second, is that of tension, which, unlike the other dimensions, increases according to the square root; that is to say, assuming a string of four pounds tension, to draw it up an octave in pitch demands an increase of tension to sixteen pounds.

There are three strings forming each note until the bass section of the scale is reached with the covered strings already mentioned. Of these there are notes of two strings in unison, and finally single strings of considerable weight, diameter, and tension; the tone thus obtained being of rounder and deeper quality than was formerly the case when notes of three unisons to the very lowest prevailed. The core wire determines the proper string vibration, to be handicapped by the covering wire which lowers the pitch by adding weight. In a modern grand piano each string alone, when drawn up to the usual pitch, requires the equivalent of a very great weight to meet the strain of its tension, and this the framing has to supply. Broadwood's normal tension in 1862 was 150 lb. avoirdupois for each string of steel wire; a strain that has of late years been much exceeded by grand pianoforte makers. Steinways construct their concert grand pianos to bear a strain of 60,000 lb.—nearly 27 tons.* In some recent concert grand pianos made by Broadwood, a tension of very nearly 30 tons has been attained; the average strain for each string at the English Philharmonic pitch being stated as 275 lb.† These instruments come up easily in tuning to the required tension: no strings giving way, although the increase is equivalent to tuning the strings of the 1862 tension a fourth higher.‡ A minor third, however, best expresses the average rise in the tension of grand pianos. It is not safe to exceed it, as the ground tone is likely to fly off.

* Steinway & Sons.—"A Brief History and Explanation of the Steinway System in Pianofortes" (New York, 1885), p. 7, mentions a possible pull of the strings of 75,000 lb., but only with reference to what their metal frame would bear. The weight given in the text is what that firm claims.
† Middle C; assumed as a mean tension for the whole scale.
‡ More than a fourth, c. 150 lb. = F 264, F♯ 300.

It may be broadly stated that the greater the tension the greater is the elasticity of the wire and consequent breaking up of vibration into smaller sections, inducing greater length of sound or *sostenente* power, with an increased clearness and brightness in the quality of the tone. The possible drawback is loss of diapason quality, that roundness and fulness due to the long smooth sections of the vibrating string which constitute the common chord with the harmonic seventh. This last interval does not enter into our modern system of music; but anyone listening to the natural music of the Æolian harp will recognise its importance in the vibrations of a string. When the high and often discordant upper partial tones are developed, they withdraw from the lower harmonious vibrating sections a richness we associate with the diapason tone of an old organ, and with this increase of tension the resisting power of the framing must be added to: the belly and bridge change their thicknesses and larger hammers are used; all these differences having to be sought for and determined empirically; there are no theoretical axioms on which to rely, the problem being too complex to be solved as yet by science. Ultimate judgment rests upon a fine sense of hearing and an accurate power of observation based upon experience. Perhaps of all musical instruments the pianoforte is, in these respects, the most complex; but the most simple instrument, whether string or wind, which substitutes a vibrating air column for the vibrating string, is amenable to this general statement.

The tension of strings is determined by a weighted monochord, the record being taken from a steelyard. Equality of tension is a desideratum in pianoforte making.

THE WREST-PLANK.

A part of a pianoforte which obtains its technical name from the old English " wrest," a tuning-hammer or key. It is the plank or block in which the wrest or tuning-pins are inserted. It is usually of beech, or beech and wainscot in thicknesses, glued together, with the grain of each wood crossing at right angles to prevent splitting. There are as many holes bored out of the plank as there are tuning-pins to drive in. Plates of metal are also used to guarantee the solidity of this part of the structure, which should, theoretically, be absolutely rigid to preserve the vibration of the strings unimpaired at the points of bearing. The wrest-pins are tighter in the holes in modern pianos than was formerly accounted necessary, to ensure their remaining immovable notwithstanding the force and frequency of the blows transmitted from the player to the strings. The rapidity with which pianos of half-a-century ago went out of tune, when the wire was less elastic and the wrest-pins less firm, would surprise a pianist of the present day. That the tuning of a grand piano had invariably to be revised between the parts of a concert is in the remembrance of some who are still living.

THE CASE AND FRAMING.

The outside of a pianoforte case is usually veneered, concealing the solid wood, which, in good instruments, may be of mahogany or oak, black walnut or other hard wood. Broadwood's grand pianos have the curved sides bent in the solid wood by steam, and afterwards veneered. Steinways build their grand piano cases of layers of continuous maple and oak, of veneer thickness and of adequate length, and bent into the required form in metal presses. Bechstein, in his latest model, has twenty-two thicknesses of wood in the curved side and end, the back being solid or in two thicknesses; it is supposed that these expedients assist the resonance. In the Steinway and Bechstein grand pianos the depth of the bent or curved side is reduced considerably. Bracings or trusses of wood are, with all pianos, strutted within the under part of the case beneath the sound-board, and are so disposed, in combination with the metal frame, as to guarantee the durability of the entire instrument against the continuous strain of the strings. They also help to maintain the tension of the sound-board against the downward pressure of the bridge. The cases of good pianos are so accurately designed and made, that there is a very slight difference in the levels taken before and after an instrument has been strung and drawn up to the required pitch. It is an elastic framing that is sought for, rather than one absolutely rigid; flexible enough to permit the sympathetic molecular vibration of the wood and metal, while providing the stiffness of thrust and resistance required for the necessary strength of the structure.

Pianofortes, up to the year 1820, were, like spinets, harpsichords, and clavichords, entirely wooden structures—always increasing in solidity, as time went on, in proportion to an ever increasing tension. The weakest part was always at the treble end. To obviate this weakness was a problem for the pianoforte maker—at one time, it would seem, almost insuperable. A new era was inaugurated when metal was added to wood in piano structure. It was a problem not to be solved by any one inventor, but rather by many who, in their turn, added to the building up of the newer and stronger instrument. Theobald Boehm, whose name is associated with the modern flute, and whose suggestions for the piano as well as music wire were far from unimportant, wrote in a letter to an English friend: "If it were desirable to analyse all the inventions which have been brought forward, we should find that in scarcely any instance were they the offspring of the brain of a single individual; but that all progress is gradual only, each worker following in the track of his predecessor and eventually, perhaps, advancing a step beyond him." Three men, however, may have that originality claimed for them which Boehm's proposition hardly allows, in metal framing for pianos: John Isaac Hawkins, an Englishman at one time residing in America; William Allen, a Scotchman; and Alpheus Babcock, an American. Not one of these three had a predecessor, so far as is known, in his inventions.

The iron frame applied to a piano by John Isaac Hawkins antedates my starting-point by twenty years. As we shall give attention to this remarkable man when concerned with the history of the upright piano, and his invention was, at the time, unappreciated and in after years nearly forgotten, I name him here only with reference to originality. A contemporary invention by Joseph Smith, patented in London in 1799,* of iron bracings or struts, which preceded, and possibly led up to the iron bars of modern instruments, was not intended for this important use, but to economise the space occupied by wood bracings, increased by Smith's invention to admit of the introduction of a drum or tambourine behind the belly; the German pianos of that day making their drum pedal for Janissary music by an apparatus beating against the belly itself. James Shudi Broadwood tried iron bars to resist the treble strain in 1808, and again in 1818, but was not successful in fixing them.

* Joseph Smith, No. 2,315.

The real change from a wooden resisting structure to one in which iron should play an important part is due to William Allen, a tuner, who was in the employ of Stodart, one of the leading pianoforte makers at that time in London. Allen conceived the idea of a metal system of framing, intended by him to meet the disturbance in tuning caused by the strings being of two metals, brass and iron, which were differently influenced by change of temperature. With the co-operation of Stodart's foreman, Thom, the invention was completed and a patent taken out in their joint names, James Thom and William Allen, on January 15, 1820.* It was at once bought of them by the Stodart firm. The patent was for a combination of parallel metal tubes, with metal plates, iron over the iron strings, and brass over the brass and spun strings in the bass division of the instrument; the metal plates grooved to slide upon balls fixed to the bent side, and holding the hitch-pins to which the farther ends of the strings were attached. The strings becoming less tense by heat and consequently flatter in pitch, it was supposed that the lengthening of the tubes, owing to the same cause, would, by extending the bearings of the strings, effect an adequate compensation. Stout wooden bars, crossing the tubes at right angles, guaranteed the stability of the tubing. At once a great advance was made in the possibility of using thicker and heavier strings, and the great merit of the invention was universally acknowledged; but not so much on account of compensation, as of resistance against the strain of the strings. The next step was towards a fixed string-plate, and was due to one of Broadwood's workmen, Samuel Hervé. This was in 1821, when it was introduced by that firm in their square pianos. In 1822 Sebastian and Pierre Erard patented in Paris a complete system of nine iron bars from treble to bass, with fastenings piercing the bars, and through apertures in the belly to the wooden bracings beneath. There was no metal plate in this patent, nor was such a plate included in the same firm's London patent of 1824, which chiefly concerned their repetition action. In fact, neither Erard nor Broadwood could claim the invention of bars in the United Kingdom while Stodart's patent was in force. William Stodart, however generously consented to overlook any advantage taken of the patent by his competitors, so that there was really no hindrance to the development of the idea of fixed iron framing by those who could

* James Thom and William Allen, No. 4,431.

advance it. James Shudi Broadwood, in 1827, combined the metal string-plate with fixed metal bars and took out a patent* for this important invention, one feature of which was the entire control gained over the unused lengths of wire behind the belly-bridge. The wood and iron pianoforte was now brought to its first stage of efficiency. There were four bars in Broadwood's patent, but no bar parallel with the straight side and lowest bass string. Erard had nine bars, including a bass bar; afterwards reducing the number. The bars were strutted from fastenings upon the wrest-plank to a block of wood that held the further fastenings of the strings, technically hitch-pins; later to Broadwood's metal plate which held the hitch-pins and defined the farther ends or fastenings of the strings. The space required for the bars to pass cramped and divided the scale, an obvious drawback. It has also been troublesome to adjust the bars for each one to bear a proportionate share of the strain. Their accurate fitting is, therefore, of great importance.

William Allen was the author of another invention in framing, patented in 1831,† that, less fortunate than his first invention, led to no practical result. It was anticipated, although it appears to have been an independent invention, by the American patent of Babcock, which will be presently described. Allen proposed to apply to the pianoforte a cast-iron frame, and a special feature of this framing was that it was grooved for wrest-pin bars of wood, to be tightly driven in, secured by glue, and veneered over. Then the holes were to be made for the wrest-pins, which were expected to be more firmly held, and consequently less likely to move from the force of playing. In short, an idea that has been carried out in respect to tightness in the modern wrest-pins.

Pierre Erard introduced the harmonic bar. It is a bar of brass or gun-metal or nickel, placed upon the wrest-plank near its edge, immediately above the bearings of the treble strings, consolidating the plank by means of screws tapped into it, of alternate pressure and drawing power. By this bar a more ringing and clear tone was gained for the treble, the bearing points being firmer. It is not, however, indispensable.

Henry Fowler Broadwood set himself the problem of still further reducing the iron bars. His aim was to get rid of them altogether, but in this he was not successful. He reduced the number of the

* James Shudi Broadwood, No. 5,985. † William Allen, No. 6,140.

steel "arches" or struts fixed between the wrest-plank and the belly-bar, a wooden transverse bar against which the belly is supported. In 1847-9 he succeeded in making a grand piano with an entire upper framing of iron, and in this instrument two bars sufficed, neither breaking into the scale, one parallel with the lowest bass string along the straight side of the instrument, the other presenting the entirely new feature of a diagonal bar, fixed at the bass corner of the wrest-plank and again on the string-plate, and having its thrust at an angle to the pull of the strings. But in the grand pianos he afterwards made with his diagonal bar, he also used a straight bar towards the treble, of the ordinary type, to avoid any possible sacrifice to durability. This was the Broadwood Iron Grand Model of 1851—the first to be made in England in a complete iron framing, but not solid; it was in wrought and cast-iron, wedged up with gun-metal at the points of juncture, and not in a single casting as is the American plan.

Nearly simultaneous with Allen's invention of tubes and plates was the not less important conception of a cast iron frame in which to fix a square piano, an invention of the American pianoforte maker, Alpheus Babcock. His invention comprised a complete metal frame with a hitch-pin plate, made in one casting. He patented it at Boston, Massachusetts, U.S.A., December 17, 1825. It was not as many have thought, including at one time myself, a compensation frame, but one intended from the first for resistance. I will quote from the late Daniel Spillane* an extract from the records of the Franklin Institute, Philadelphia, relating to the pianos shown at the fourth annual exhibition in October, 1827:—
"Expecially mention is made of a horizontal piano by A. Babcock, of Boston, of an *improved construction*, the frame which supports the strings being of *solid cast-iron* and strong enough to resist their enormous tension." Babcock removed from Boston to Philadelphia in December, 1829, and began manufacturing there. It would appear that he also took out a patent at Philadelphia for an almost identical iron framing for a square piano, except that there were three bars for resistance instead of one. That in the treble part of the scale was in both patents, and two were added lower down in the latter. But the patent, dated May 24, 1830, is described as for

* Spillane, Daniel, "**History of the American Pianoforte**" (New York, 1890), pp. 122-3 and 364.

"cross-stringing pianofortes." Unfortunately the original record was destroyed by fire in 1836. If Babcock intended overstringing by this term, he conceived both the principles that in combination characterise the modern American pianoforte.

Another maker in Philadelphia, Conrad Meyer, modified this iron framing in 1832-3, abolishing the bars; he did not, possibly could not, patent it, but he exhibited his instrument at the Franklin Institute in 1833, and showing it or one similar to it at the Centennial Exhibition at Philadelphia, in 1876, and the Paris Exhibition of 1878, he, or his representatives, claimed the invention. But Babcock preceded him, and it is difficult to understand that Meyer could have made and sold pianos in iron frames at that time without an agreement with Babcock.

Jonas Chickering, of Boston, carried this invention much farther: he patented, in 1840, a new iron frame for square pianos.* As well as the frame there was, in this patent, a long bar parallel with the bass strings. In this casting there is a greater economy of space combined with increased strength, and there is also, cast with it, a fixed damper rail. The culmination of Jonas Chickering's achievement in this direction was his grand piano frame in one solid casting, patented in 1843.† He could not claim the upward bearing at the wrest-plank by means of agraffes (Sebastian Erard's invention—little detached bridges for each note, the strings passing through holes in them and bearing upwards); but Chickering did claim casting this bearing as a solid ledge, the strings passing through openings in it the same as in the agraffes. The solid cast plate for a grand piano was, however, the principal object of his patent. Before proceeding to Steinway & Sons' grand piano it is necessary to place before the student in pianoforte history the various claimants in Europe and America for the invention of "overstringing," that plan by which the bass or over-spun strings are carried over the long steel strings at another angle, thereby gaining greater length for them, and, at the same time, permitting a wider scale. Spillane's claim for the Englishman, Thomas Loud, in 1802, cannot be accepted on the plea that diagonal and parallel mean diagonal and vertical, and we have no other claimant prior to 1830, when Babcock's patent, already referred to, was taken out in Philadelphia for "cross-stringing pianofortes." An almost

* Spillane, pp. 92 and 364.   † Ibid, p. 92.

simultaneous suggestion appears to have come from Theobald Boehm, the reconstructor of the flute, who, in a letter written by him, June 21, 1867, to Mr. W. S. Broadwood,* says that, in 1831, he advised Gerock & Wolf, of 79, Cornhill, London, as to the desirability of overstrung scales. I have found that in 1835 a cabinet, a smaller upright or piccolo, and a square piano had been made by that firm according to Boehm's design, all overstrung. But quite independently, a square piano was made and exhibited in New York, in 1833, by Bridgeland & Jardine, the latter claiming the invention, in which the bass strings are said to have "crossed over the treble." In point of fact, two square pianos were made by Mr. John Jardine in that year, with overstrung basses, the particulars of which are recorded in Spillane's book.† These are believed to have been the first overstrung pianos made in America. Pape was undoubtedly the first to introduce overstringing in French pianos, and from an English patent, granted to Pierre Frederick Fischer, in 1835, in which overstringing and the employment of felt for hammers‡ appear, the inference is that Pape was Fischer's friend, who inspired the patent from abroad. In 1836 there was another English patent, bearing the name of John Godwin, who claimed the invention of overstringing as his own; his invention consisting in "a new arrangement of the strings in square, and in cottage, and in piccolo pianofortes, in which some of the strings are stretched or placed across or obliquely over lines or directions in which the others are stretched or placed."§ In square pianos, on this principle, an improvement is made in the upper or treble notes " by opening the scale and producing a fuller and a more perfect tone; and in cottage and piccolo pianofortes an improvement is made in the bass and lower octaves by allowing greater length for the bass or lower strings." A few years later Tomkison, a well known London pianoforte maker in his time,

---

* The translator of "Boehm on the Flute." London, 1882. The letter of Theobald Boehm says: "With reference to your brother's question, the matter stands thus: Mr. Wolf and I were already very intimate friends when I came, in 1831, for the first time to London. As Mr. Gerock was making very bad pianos I sought out Wolf to improve them. Among many projects of mine one was to cross the bass strings or lay them obliquely. Mr. Gerock was against it because it disturbed the action and cost more. Later on I found it often enough applied."

† Spillane, p. 158.

‡ P. F. Fischer, No. 6,835.

§ John Godwin, No. 7,021

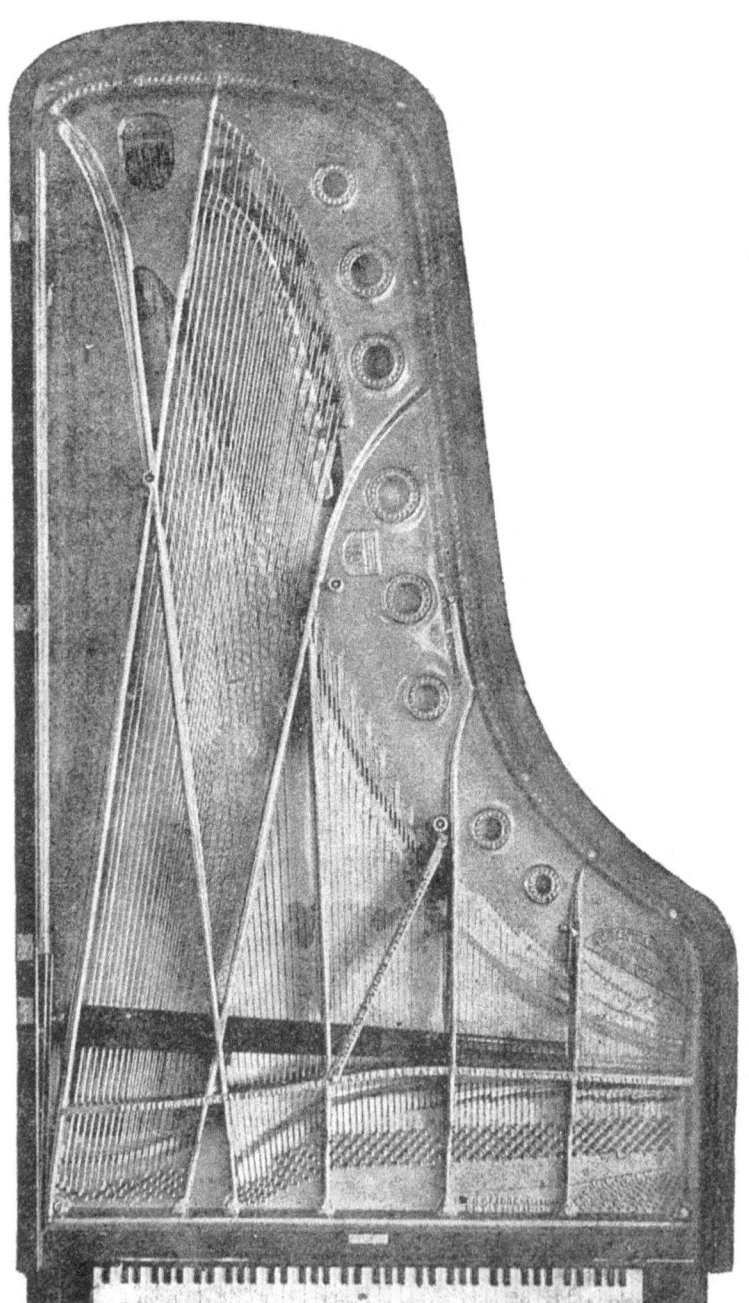
CONCERT GRAND PIANOFORTE BY STEINWAY AND SONS, NEW YORK AND HAMBURG, 1895.

produced a grand and a cottage piano according to Godwin's patent; it is probable that he made more.

I do not overlook the fact that there were, in the eighteenth century, overstrung clavichords, giving by this contrivance extra length to a few of the lowest bass strings. It is not now possible to say how far a knowledge of this clavichord overstringing may have suggested the earliest attempts at overstringing pianofortes, if it suggested them at all.

Among the rival claimants to the invention there is certainly some confusion; there is no doubt the idea was in the air at the time, but years passed by before it came prominently under public notice. In the 1851 Exhibition in Hyde Park there was an overstrung grand piano exhibited, with separate sound-boards, answering to the respective diagonal scales, made by Lichtenthal, of St. Petersburg.* His object was not so much to extend his scale as to make a symmetrical grand piano with two curved sides instead of one straight and one curved, as is usual with grand pianos.

We now come to the grand piano of Steinway & Sons, of New York—an invention patented by Henry Engelhard Steinway in that city, December 20, 1859†—anticipated in a similarly made square piano, exhibited for the first time at the American Institute in New York in 1855. The grand piano was played upon in public, for the first time, at the New York Academy of Music, on February 8, 1859. It is hardly necessary to say the square piano, as an instrument, has been for years superseded by the grand and upright pianos. With respect to Steinway's invention—in its broad features the combination of a solid metal frame and overstringing—there can be no doubt it represents the flood-mark of American pianoforte making; what has been done since being to modify and further improve it according to the ideas and experience of the respective makers of different countries who have adopted it. In overstrung grand pianos a great display of ironwork is to be seen; the whole of the inside frame, including the agraffe ledge, is in a single casting, and the bars and scale are so adjusted as to overstring the bass at an angle which opens out in a double curve fan shape from the hammer striking-place down to the hitch-pins (in square pianos it was the reverse) and allow an increased

* Catalogue of the Great Exhibition, London, 1851, No. 1,172.
† Steinway & Sons, p. 3; and Spillane, pp. 217-219, and pp. 364-367.

width to the belly or sounding-board. One of the most important results of complete iron framing is an increase of tension, rendered possible by the tenacity of the modern cast steel wire. In upright pianos the single casting has become universal, and overstringing (sometimes double overstringing) prevails in the larger upright instruments of America and Germany. The tendency to be feared is that pianoforte making may become mechanical from the fixity implied by systems of casting, but owing to the tighter straining of the strings, in combination with the influence exerted by masses of iron in large castings, there is obtained in the pianoforte a more *sostenente* or singing tone, and the instrument stands longer in tune.

Let me emphasize that in none of these constructions is the under wooden frame superseded. It still remains in American and German pianos, as in French and English, in combination with the case the foundation of the instrument. The illustrations show the metal framings employed in the latest concert grand pianos of Broadwood and Steinway, and are sufficient to explain to the eye the difference between parallel and overstringing. I might have added further illustrations to show the divergent patterns of metal barring of Collard, Erard, Bechstein, Blüthner, and other eminent makers,* and have also included upright pianos; but assuming that so far as upright pianos are concerned the greater includes the less, and in grand pianos that there is no variation from one or the other design that is not self-explanatory, my purpose is served by the examples I give. Concert grands approach nine feet in length; the largest made is the "Imperial" concert grand of Bösendorfer, Vienna, an overstrung piano nearly ten feet in length (2·92 mètres), and with a keyboard compass of eight octaves ($\underline{\underline{F}}$—$e^5$).

The latest radical alteration of construction is to be found in Broadwood's barless pianoforte, a patent for which was taken out by Mr. Henry John Tschudi Broadwood, January 26, 1888.† The metal plate is here of mild or cast steel turned up round the sides to form a continuous flange, so as to meet the strain without requiring bars; going back, in fact, in simplicity of construction to the original wooden pianos *ante* 1820, but adequately bearing the modern

---

* The leading pianoforte makers of the world are named by Professor Ernst Pauer in "A Dictionary of Pianists and Composers for the Pianoforte, with an Appendix of Manufacturers." London: Novello & Co., 1895.

† H. J. Tschudi Broadwood, No. 1,231.

increase of tension. It is an ideal construction, and the musical instrument thus produced is of singular beauty and equality of tone.

It is an often repeated question of decorative artists if the lines and curves of grand pianos could not be improved so as to make them as the sixteenth and seventeenth century harpsichords were, pleasing objects to the eye?* The solution of this question is more difficult with the overstrung than with the parallel-strung grand pianos, and with both the modern excessive width of the keyboard is a serious obstacle. While, however, it is easy to design lines whether rectilinear or curved that shall be agreeable to the eye, the engineering problems of stress and strain, and the pianoforte makers' quest of tone quality and quantity have all to be considered. The question of the legs or supports can be easier dealt with, but they must be strong enough and allow of the instrument being moved without lifting. The cabinet or console shape of the upright piano, like that of the grand piano, was determined when the invention took place, and gives no sanction to the meretricious adornment very often put upon it. Extending the dimensions of the upright instrument unduly is disadvantageous to the shape, which is seen at its best in the little pianette.

Before passing on to the next division of my subject, I have to refer to those expedients in scaling which are intended to excite sympathetic vibrations.† Steinway's " Duplex scale " is a scaling or measuring off into proportionate lengths of the unused wire on the hither and farther sides of the bridges, between which are the vibrating lengths amenable to the impulse of the hammers. The " duplex " scalings vibrate from influence, or sympathetically. They extend in Steinway's latest grand model from d^2 in the treble clef upwards, giving corresponding sympathetic notes in accordance with their length, graduating from the double or superoctave, the

---

* "Dictionary of Music and Musicians" (A. J. H.), Vol. III., p. 656. An attempt was made in the early days of the pianoforte (1782), by Crang Hancock, to build one in the pleasing wing shape of the English spinet; but the result was not such as to induce imitation, nor with the present conception of the instrument would it be advisable to repeat the experiment, as some impressed with the often graceful lines of the spinet desire.

† See Adlung, "Musica Mechanica Organoedi, Zweiter Band," S. 154, Berlin, 1768, for the recognition of the value sympathetically of unused lengths of string, even with the clavichord; and a letter of Duarte, written in 1648, concerning the inventions of Jan Couchet, quoted *in extenso* under " Harpsichord."

twelfth, the octave, the fifth, and, finally, the unison equivalents. On the hither side of the wrest-plank bearing the accession of sympathetic vibration is less noticeable. Other eminent makers have not accepted this aid. As a directly opposite instance Bechstein places his metal string-plate as near as possible to the belly-bridge to get rid of unused wire.

Blüthner's "Aliquot" scale supplies sympathetic octave strings, on their own sound-board bridge, away from the contact of the hammer; adding a fourth string to each note so dealt with. The octave notes extend from the upper g of the bass clef to g^2 above the treble clef. After that note, for the rest of the scale upwards, the untouched strings are tuned in unison with the notes they are attached to. The octave is the strongest partial tone in the composite note, even without this sympathetic addition.

THE BELLY OR SOUND-BOARD.

The belly, sound-board, or sounding-board is the resonance factor or medium by which the weak sound of the strings is reinforced, so as to become audible and intensified to a satisfactory impression of tone-quantity. The increase is, in the first place, due to the width of this elastic table which is, over all its surface, in immediate contact with the surrounding air. The substance of the strings is too slender to cause more than an excitement of the air in their immediate vicinity. Yet all the characteristic quality of tone is already present in this feeble sound, even to the most complex figures of vibration. The pulsations are passed on through a hardwood bridge, glued down upon the belly, and the fibres of the bellywood take them up faithfully and extend them to the utmost that the dimensions and barring of the belly will allow; reproducing them, less any absorption there may be through imperfect material or communication, but with absolutely no addition to the vibrational figures. As this problem is difficult to express and may be hard to understand, I will mention two simple experiments. One is to place the stem of a vibrating tuning-fork upon the belly-bridge; the reinforced tone will be tuning-fork tone, no other. Or, take out the front of an upright piano, and with the dampers removed from the strings by means of the pedal, sing the different vowels in notes

CROSS-STRUNG CONCERT GRAND PIANO BY BROADWOOD 1896 SHOWING THE BELLY-BARS.

agreeing with the pitch of the instrument. You will hear in response from the sound-board, set into vibration through the strings and bridge, the vowel sung, unobscured in the transmission.

Let it be remembered that the elasticity of the wood forming the sound-board, even when strengthened by barring, is small in comparison with that of the cast steel wire strings at the enormous tension to which they are tuned; it is entirely controlled and its proper note absorbed by the stronger factor.

In England, France, and Germany pianoforte bellies are made of Spruce Fir (*Abies excelsa*), in that regular growth that is known in the musical instrument trade as Swiss Pine. The best firwood for the purpose is, however, no longer Swiss, but comes from the more Eastern mountain ranges of Europe. The resin in the wood should be in equally and regularly distributed channels. The vibratory substance is the fibrous wood which is between the streaks of resin, and as in course of time the resin dries the fibres gain in vibrating elasticity, a material change which accounts for the more responsive and mellow tone of some old instruments. The wood has become lighter as well as more elastic. The tree being, when cut, of considerable width, the boards are evenly broad that are used to make up a belly, and the joinings should be faultless. The thickness employed is usually from a quarter to three-eighths of an inch, and is reduced towards the edges. The direction of the grain, as well as disposition of the strengthening bars which should accord with it, rests with the choice and experience of the maker. In America another variety of fir is used, the *Abies Alba*. Of course, other woods of regular grain might be employed, as cypress was by the Italians for their spinets. General consent has, however, awarded the preference to the fir, on account of its light specific gravity and its superior elasticity. This last quality is assisted and intensified by the practice of the barring above-mentioned: glueing batons of the same or sometimes a heavier wood against the back of the belly. The batons are an inch or more in thickness, and are disposed with a two-fold object: to maintain the level of the belly, which is, or should be, put in slightly convex to resist the downward pressure of the bridge; and to impart to it a greater tension and higher elasticity, so as to promote the formation of nodes—*i.e.*, *foci*—where crossing lines of vibration meet. The nodes, as already said in reference to the strings, are apparently points of rest; but are really points of concentration, escaping from which the vibrations resume their activity. The principles underlying the bellying of pianos and the barring, which may be called the nervous system of the piano, are common to all musical instruments having strings and sound-boards. These principles were understood before the piano was invented; the early spinet makers having evolved them from the primitive barrings of the lute and similar instruments. The great width of a piano increases the difficulty of the barring, and the solution can only be experimental, depending upon those finer appreciations of hearing and proportion upon which success in musical instrument-making attends.

On the American principle of pianoforte-making the belly is independent of the case, and is secured upon the interior rim of the wooden frame or case, and the cross-beam or belly-bar. The edge of it beneath the metal plate is, by Steinway, submitted to the action of external screws intended to give a continuous pressure sideways against the edge or rim of the sound-board.

To return to the particular service rendered by the belly or sound-board: a good one reproduces all figures of vibration, however complex, as freely and surely as they are reproduced by the surrounding air; but, like the air, it is an indifferent conductor of sound. The vibrations ceasing with their cause, we have not to endure the mixture of sound as in the tone of a gong or bell in its prolongation, due to bell-metal having much greater conducting power than wood, or atmospheric air, which has even less than wood.

The idea of an auxiliary sound reinforcer finds its latest exposition in the Piano Resonator, patented by Daniel Mayer,* which consists of a sheet of manganese steel wherein are cut slits, the edges of which are turned over to form half-tubes open to the sound-board bars. It is attached at the back of the upright piano and underneath the grand, and covers the entire superficies. It is fastened to the case by clips and screws. The essential attachment between the belly bars and the half-tubes is effected by silken cords which are tense. The entire Resonator has a gong-like reverberation of its own—a deep note which may vary half a tone or more according to contact. The superior energy of the piano strings and sound-board overcomes this note. Owing to the metal it produces an

* No. 1,820, January 25, 1896.

agreeably reedy and more sustained tone, due to the continued vibration of the higher partials or vibrating divisions of the string. This is naturally less audible in the treble. Being an addition it somewhat increases the power. It can be fixed to instruments of any shape or make.

The originality of this invention is in the material being metal, the tubing, and the connection by tension with the belly-bars. These distinguish it from the double sound-boards, patents for which have not been infrequent since the first which was recorded in 1783.* In their use sound-posts have been mainly relied upon, but no ingenuity has yet been able to maintain the vitality of a principle which, necessary in violins and similar instruments, has not commended itself in the piano, and has soon been passed by and forgotten. The nearest approach to a tensile connection has been Cadby's patent of 1857,† wherein there were springs, not absolutely tense and probably inefficient. While the double sound-board patents have been chiefly dependent upon vibratory influence—in other words, sympathetic vibration—in Mr. Mayer's Resonator there is a mechanical coercion which separates it from previous attempts to modify or add vibration by auxiliary sound-boards. But our living rooms are no less resonators, modifying tone by resonance or absorption due to their proportions, to their walls, floors, and furniture, and also to the people in them who displace their equivalent in vibrating air.

THE BRIDGES.

These are the wrest-plank bridge, agraffes (separate stud bridges) or pressure bar, regulating the higher bearing of the strings, and the belly-bridge (or bridges), regulating the further bearing of the lengths vibrating from the concussion of the hammers. The belly-bridge is the true bridge by which the oscillations of the strings are carried down to the sound-board. It is of hard wood, such as beech, or, according to the practice of some makers, of alternate layers of different woods overlaid with a veneering of boxwood. Hard wood where the strings lie is shown, empirically,

* John Broadwood, No. 1,379.
† Charles Cadby, No. 2,719.

to be indispensable. With divided bridges the longer division of the belly-bridge carries the steel strings from the treble to their limit downwards, while the shorter division is for the bass or overspun strings. In overstrung pianos the bass bridge is behind the long bridge carrying the steel strings. Steinways return this long bridge so as to form a back bridge, and call it, when thus extended, a "ring" bridge. The double pinning observable on the belly-bridge is intended to stop off on the one side the vibrating length of the string, and, on the other, to guide it without jarring to the toneless, or, it may be, "duplex"—*i.e.*, aliquot vibrating—remainder between the bridge and the hitch-pins.

The wrest-plank bridge, under whatever form it may occur, is the true nut, *capotasto*, or head fret, from which the vibrating length of string starts. It may be of wood, pinned like the belly-bridge, the blow of the hammer in a grand piano driving the strings upwards away from their bearing; or it may be a metal agraffe or stud—that is to say, a little separate nut provided for each group of unison strings, the hammer driving them upwards to their bearing; or it may be a long so-called Capotasto (head fret), or, corruptly, Capo d'Astro—bar of metal, a pressure bar—the invention of the late Antoine Bord, a French pianoforte maker, worked to a blunt edge, which presses upon the strings collectively on the line of bearing, and performs the same duty as the other expedients mentioned—viz., to divide the vibrating length from the unused wire on the hither side in a grand, or upper side in an upright piano, nearer the wrest or tuning-pins.

THE ACTION.

We have now briefly surveyed the structure forming the instrument: the strings, wrest-plank, case and framing, the belly, and the bridges. Yet no sound is forthcoming but such as can be incited by chipping the strings with the extremities of the finger nails, as an Irish harp was played; or by blows of hammers held in the hands, as with the dulcimer, the precursor of the piano.

To make the instrument a pianoforte we need, with the hammers, the keyboard and the mechanical apparatus, which comprising key and hammer we call the action—the mechanical movement that transmits the impetus given by the player's touch to the strings. With this is included the damper to stop the sound.

The keyboard is, in modern pianos, of seven octave compass, A—A, or seven octaves and a minor third, A—C, and the width of the octave, with all makers, and without respect of country, is so nearly the same that a player should hardly be incommoded by any difference of stretch of the fingers. The extremities of this wide compass are very near the average limits of the human ear to appreciate and distinguish musical sounds. A key is a jack, or lever, centred upon a pin driven into a wooden balance rail, which pin is held in a mortise bored through the key, the deviation from a true balance being controlled by the insertion of pellets of lead in the wood, usually lime tree, which is used by the best makers for keys on account of its not warping. Another pin is held in a mortise beneath the key in front, and is intended to prevent too much lateral movement, by which the keys might strike each other and cause a rattling noise. The mortises are often lined with cloth or felt with the same object. The lower keys are called the naturals and, where seen, are covered with ivory; the visible ends of the shorter upper keys, called sharps, are raised to the height required by blocks of ebony glued upon them. The balancing of these shorter keys is designed to agree with the longer, but in practice the player alters the balance according to the backward or forward position of the fall of the finger upon the key, as may be convenient for the position of the hand. By shortening the distance from the centre of the key-lever the weight is increased. In playing in different scales and the various chords it is not possible to attack each key for the same note at the identical point of leverage. There is thus an ever recurring divergence in weight. The player rectifies this defect by scale practice, and for the most part unconsciously, in the same way that the stronger and weaker fingers are worked by practice towards a level equality of touch. A trial of the weight required to produce the faintest *pianissimo* in one of Broadwood's concert grand pianos with repetition action, gives approximately for

Lowest A	Middle C	Highest C
3¼ oz.	2¾ oz.	2 oz.

Touching the key farther back, as already said, increases the weight in proportion as the distance of the lever from the centre is shortened.

The piano keyboards in the first thirty or forty years of the century, following the fashion of the older spinets and harpsichords, were made with shorter ivory head-pieces than now prevail; the ebony sharps and ivory tail-pieces were also shorter. The position of the player's hand was therefore different, the thumb not being held so much above the natural keys, but rather in front of them, and the fingers attacking them nearer to the front edge. The wear being more confined to one spot, the ivory became hollowed out, and even the front edge was occasionally destroyed, as may be seen in old pianos that have been much used. The modern position of the hands being more over the keyboard, with greater liberty of attack, the wear of the keys is more distributed and shows less. The hammers are attached to shanks of a light wood, such as pear tree, hickory, or white beech; tenacious, so as not to break with the hardest blow the hammer can be made to give, and yet elastic enough to rebound. Cedar has been much used for hammer-shanks on account of its elasticity, but cannot be guaranteed from fracture. The wooden head of the hammer is covered with felt, of compressed sheep's wool—in modern pianos cut from one piece, graduated in thickness from the bass to the treble, the greatest thickness and weight being in the bass. The felt must neither be too hard nor too soft; but as the precise degree of surface texture suitable for the tone of the instrument is rarely to be found, recourse has to be had to the tone regulator's needles to break this surface up for the required quality of tone. The stronger the blow given by the hammer, the greater is the velocity and the consequent increase of vibrating sections in the string, the sections diminishing in length as they increase in number. From this it arises that notes struck with force are harder, it may be harsher, in quality of tone than those produced by a slower impulse of the hammer. A hammer with a hard surface, as has been shown by Helmholtz,[*] quits the string at once after contact with it and does not damp the very dissonant upper partial tones, but lets them run their course. A hammer with a soft surface clings for a slightly longer space of time to the string and damps such discordant upper partials. The difference in contact is too short to measure; it is, however, sufficient to leave the longer and more harmonious aliquot divisions of the string continuing in

[*] Helmholtz, second English Edition, p. 75.

vibration. The extremes of these qualities of tone are often designated brilliant or mellow. Also, the larger hammers used in the bass of the instrument remain longer in contact with the string; the lighter, in the treble, having a proportionately shorter period of contact, favour a ringing tone. A worn hammer, by harder surface, produces harder tone-quality; it may, however, be somewhat tempered by the surface of the worn hammer-head being cut into by the strings and lengthened by the wearing down of the almond-shaped apex of the hammer, the ridges of felt left so raised damping them at their sides, while the flattened shape of the hammer-head favours a musical quality of tone in soft playing that distinguishes many good pianos when the hammers are nearly worn out, a charm that is frequently lost, at least for a time, when new hammers are substituted. Through this change a repaired piano not unfrequently causes disappointment, a certain charm of singing quality of tone having gone, but perhaps to return when the hammer has become again sufficiently worn. The damper is an essential part of the action intended to allow the player to stop the vibration of a note at will by simply letting the key rise to its level and position of rest. When placed beneath the strings of a grand piano, or below the line of the hammers in an upright one, it is called an "under-damper." This kind of damper requires a spring for its return to the strings. When acting from above the strings or hammers it is an "over-damper," and in the grand piano falls by its own weight. It may be also a "wedge-damper," as in Bechstein's grand pianos, when it drops between the strings forming a note instead of upon them. The damper, like the check, was included in Cristofori's invention of the pianoforte. Its function is of great importance, as will be more particularly shown when we arrive at a description of the pedals.

The action is the mechanical transmitter of the player's touch. There have been various kinds of action, some of which have only become obsolete in the last thirty years. They are now generally reduced to three models, omitting those small features of change or adaptation which are characteristic of the maker but not of the class of mechanism, and are known as the single escapement grand, the double escapement grand, and the upright or cottage check action. The first is the so-called English action, the direct lever action brought to perfection by the Broadwoods; the second comprises the Erard repetition action and a simplified form of it first introduced in the Herz pianos (Paris) and now generally known as the Herz-Erard action; the third, the modern upright action, based upon the invention of Hawkins, but owing its present form almost entirely to the English maker Wornum, who patented his model of it in 1826.* Pleyel introduced Wornum's action into Paris, and from thence it has come into general use wherever upright pianos are made; it is, however, only in the last ten years that the unchecked leather hinge sticker action, which Southwell adopted in his cabinet piano of 1807, has gone entirely out of use in this country, and the checked lever upright action gained entire possession of the field. In all these actions there are certain general features which they have necessarily in common—keys, hammers, dampers, some kind of leverage, some kind of check, or an attempt at a substitute for one to obviate a too great drop of the hammer; but whatever the mechanical contrivance may be it can always be classed among those mentioned, only with minor differences due to the conception of the maker regarding touch and the requirements of his patrons.

The following diagrams of the various actions referred to in the preceding paragraph will illustrate their mechanical intention. Broadwood's grand piano action (English direct lever action):

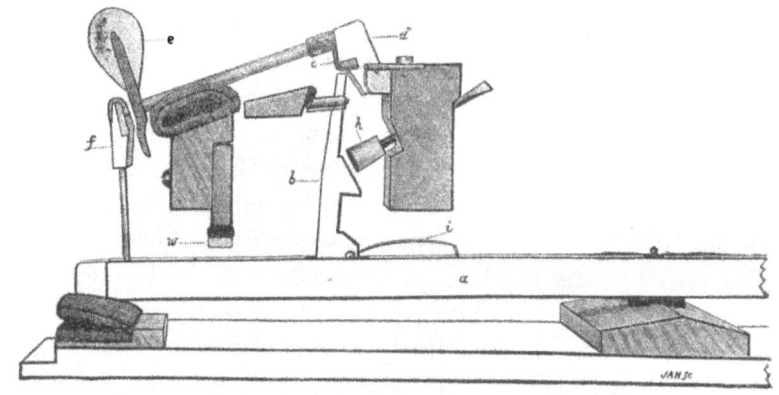

GRAND PIANOFORTE ACTION (ENGLISH ACTION), JOHN BROADWOOD AND SONS, LONDON, 1895.

the key *a*, on being depressed, raises the hopper *b*, which strikes in a notch *c*, cut in the butt of the hammer *d*. It is the play of the

* "Encyclopædia Britannica," Ninth Edition, Vol. XIX., Art. "Pianoforte" (A. J. H.), p. 75. A. & C. Black, Edinburgh, 1885.

hopper against this notch that determines the velocity of the hammer and whatever is individual from the player's touch. The hammer head is *e*. The check, which is also raised when the key is depressed, *f*, arrests the hammer in its fall, and is the first simple contrivance for repetition—that is, the possibility of the repeat of the blow of the hammer before the key returns to its equipoise; the hammer having to be raised again but a portion of its circuit. As well as the hopper and check the key raises the damper to allow the strings forming the note to continue vibrating. The damper may be over or under the strings according to choice. When under the strings the spring controlling the return of the damper adds some resistance to the touch. Escapement depends upon that space between the hammer when raised without impetus and the strings, to allow the hammer to clear them when any blow, whether soft or hard, is given. Without this provision of escapement the hammer would " block "—*i.e.*, jar against—the strings, stifling the vibration before it has time to become a musical note. The small button and screw *h* is intended, by regulating the angle of the lever, to determine the distance of the escapement, technically " set off " of the hammer from the strings, and a wire spring *i* controls the return of the hopper to its place. The damper movement is similar to those described in the subsequent paragraphs. The invention of this action dates back to about 1772, as will be told in the historical section; but the proportions of it have been modified to meet the gradual changes in pianoforte technique and construction.

Bösendorfer, of Vienna, uses the Herz-Erard action in concert grands, keeping only to the old Viennese (Streicher) action for grand pianos of lower price. Blüthner, of Leipzig, has grafted the English notch (*c* in the Broadwood action) upon an old German principle perfected by Kriegelstein, of Paris, where the escapement is made at the bottom of a centred lever or sticker raising the hammer; Blüthner merely retains the centred lever, making his escapement by the notch, with the addition of a repetition spring.*
In Germany the hopper and notch single escapement, or old Broadwood and Collard action, is known as the " English " action,†
against the " Viennese" action, now nearly obsolete. The English

* Blüthner and Gretschel, "Atlas zum Lehrbuch des Pianofortebaues" (Leipzig, no date). Diagrams: Kriegelstein, Fig. 66; Blüthner, Fig. 72.
† The double escapement Erard (Herz-Erard) action is also, although erroneously, regarded as English in Germany and Austria.

action demands higher finger movement from the player as compared with the actions about to be described, but in variety and directness of blow it is all that can be required.

The next diagram is of the Erard repetition action. The key a, when depressed, raises by a pilot, n, a lower lever or carriage, o. This lever carries the sticker or hopper b, which escapes forward, when it has delivered its thrust or blow to the nut or roller c, beneath the hammer-fork t. The roller has the same function as the notch of the English action, and the same property of transmitting to the hammer the player's intention and individuality. The hopper is centred at its base, and a prolongation, forming the escapement lever k, controls the escapement or set-off from the strings

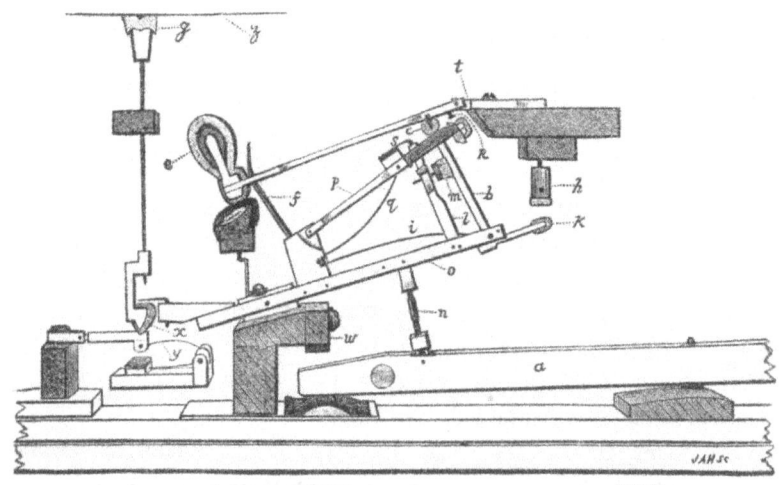

GRAND PIANOFORTE ACTION, S. AND P. ERARD, PARIS, 1895.

by the screw and button h. The lower wire spring i is the hopper spring that maintains the hopper in position, as in the English action. With the hammer-head e and the check f the first or single escapement action is complete; but a most ingenious contrivance to effect what is technically called "card"—that is, the little space required to facilitate the hopper regaining its place under the roller— is achieved by the roller resting upon the hinged upper or repetition lever p, which now comes into operation. It rises as the upper wire spring q is bent owing to the depression of the key. Through this wire repetition spring it is hardly possible to depress the key, however slowly, without producing sound. The rise of the repetition lever is dominated by a small screw r, which acts upon the point or nose of the lever, and thus causes the second escapement; the hopper falling back into its place beneath the roller before the key rises to its level. By this second escapement the hopper can repeat a blow with the key risen but a little way. There is also a metal hook s, raised upon the standard l, the use of which is precautionary, to prevent the repetition lever being forced too high. The check f is in front of the hammer instead of behind it, as in the English action. The damper g, in the Erard action, is beneath the string z. The damper lifter is x, and the spring to send it up y. The repetition or double escapement action was invented by Sebastian Erard and patented by his nephew, Pierre Erard, in 1821.

As a mechanical problem, the leading principle that governs this ingenious apparatus is counterpoise. Erard's action was long in obtaining public recognition, and an extension of the patent was obtained in 1835, on the ground of the loss that had been sustained in working it.

The Herz-Erard repetition action* is a modification and simplified form of Erard's invention, and was first introduced in the grand pianos of Henry Herz, of Paris. Its economy and efficiency have induced grand pianoforte makers, Broadwood, Collard, Steinway, Bechstein, Pleyel, and others, to use it. A version of this action used by Broadwood has been patented by a member of that firm, Mr. G. D. Rose,† and will be described as one of the latest models of the double escapement mechanism. The lower lever or carriage o is nearly unaltered in the Herz-Erard action; but the upper or repetition lever is poised upon a fork l, in which it is centred. The sticker or hopper b, the escapement prolongation k, and the button h remain the same as in the Erard action; also the springs i and q, excepting that they are separated—also the repetition screw r; but the roller c is replaced by the butt d and notch e, as in the old Broadwood action, and the stop s is shifted to the lower part of the repetition lever. The "card" described in the previous paragraph is here regulated by the button between the repetition lever and the carriage. The check f returns to its old

---

* Blüthner and Gretschel, "Atlas," Fig. 71.
† George Daniel Rose, No. 20,504, October 26, 1894.

place in the English action, behind the tail or lower part of the hammer-head *e*. Collard, while using the repetition mechanism of this action, has an additional lever which is intermediate between the hopper and roller. Rose, by substituting the notch principle for the roller gains the steadier blow of the English action, while the axes of the hammer-butts being centred upon lengths of wire, also a feature of the English action, allows of their being easier removed and cleaned when affected by damp than when each hammer axis has its own particular centre. Pleyel, Wolff and Co., of Paris, have simultaneously and quite independently arrived at a similar adaptation of these older features. Finally, *g* is the damper in this diagram, *x* the damper lifter, and *y* the damper

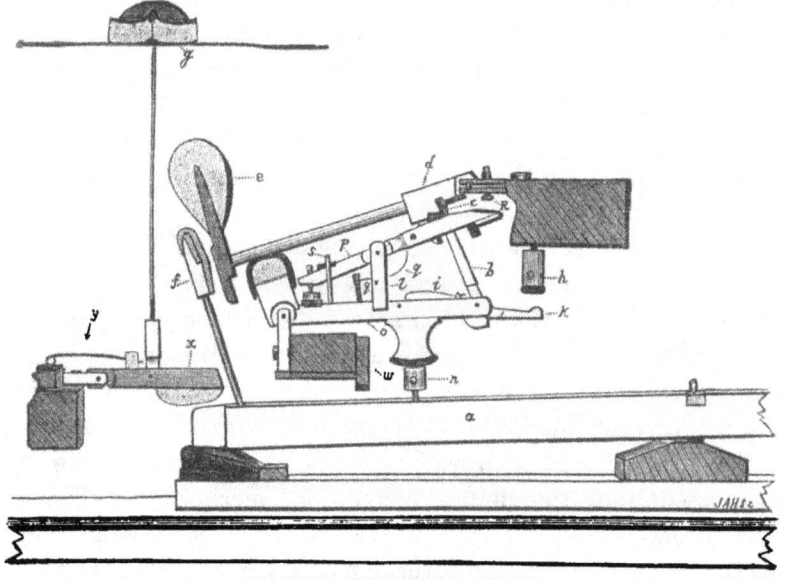

DIAGRAM, HERZ-ERARD ACTION.

spring. When an under-damper is used it resembles that in the diagram of Erard's.

We now come to the upright action, which was originally patented by Wornum in 1826, although not practically introduced in his pianos until 1829. The diagram described is Broadwood's model of that mechanism. It is hardly necessary to repeat that in making these actions there are variations, due to the intention or experience of each maker who is not a mere copyist.

a is the key, *b* the hopper, *c* the notch, *d* the hammer-butt, in

THE ACTION. 37

which is inserted the shank of *e*, the hammer-head; *f* is the check, *g* the damper, *h* is the set-off button held by a rail, *i* is the hopper spring—in this diagram the spiral spring—invented by the late A. Bord. In the actions of the higher upright instruments there is necessarily a pilot *n*, to raise the hopper and its crank to the

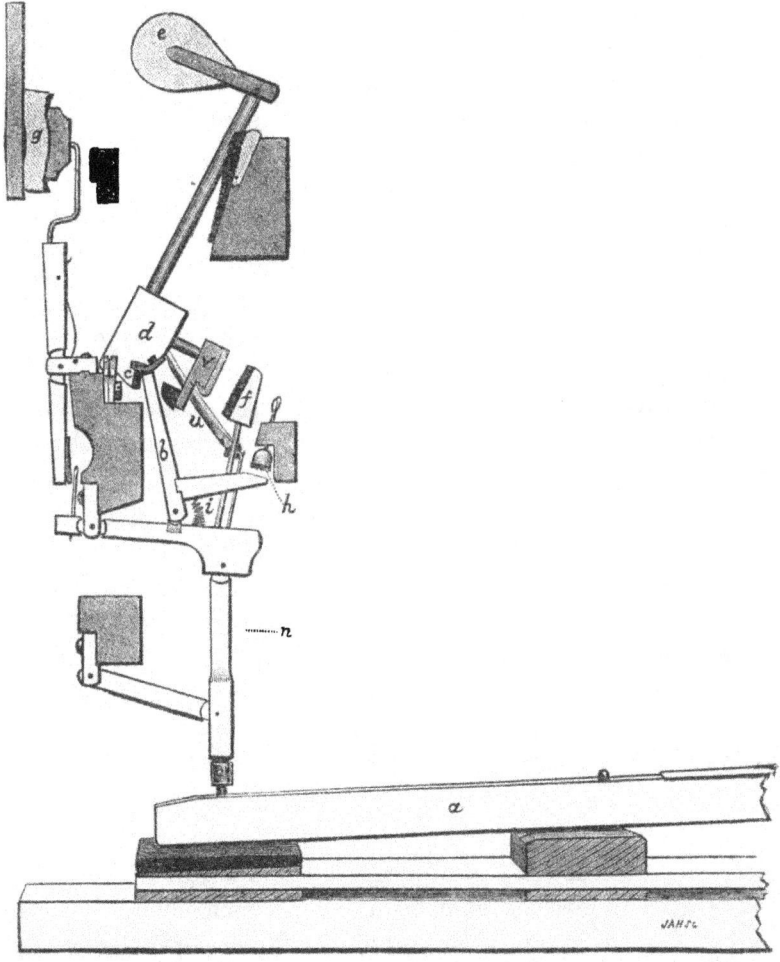

UPRIGHT PIANOFORTE ACTION, JOHN BROADWOOD AND SONS, LONDON, 1895.

height required for their service. The special merit of Wornum's invention is the tape *u*, which is tightened by the rise of the hammer when the key is struck, so as to pull the butt back, and, of course, the hammer with it, when the key returns, to assist the repetition;

the button v, projecting from the hammer-butt, falling into check, as it is called—in other words, preventing, by the contact of check and button, the hammer falling too far, the radius of the fall of the hammer always depending upon the force or velocity of blow given by the player.

In the large number of square and upright pianos formerly made that had no checks, a pad of leather behind the jack or sticker of the hopper was in some measure a substitute, a lever also clothed with leather and sometimes called an under-hammer to raise the long hinged sticker resting upon this pad. Whatever the touch may be, a certain resistance that shall be agreeable to the finger is indispensable, and particularly for playing with expression. If it is too great the touch is too heavy, if too little the touch is not only too light, but flimsy—in both cases irresponsive. Many students practise with an over weighted touch, believing that strength and facility in playing on ordinary instruments are thus secured. If so, it may be with danger to the sensitiveness of touch and to the control of gradation of tone, the pianist's chief claims to interest. Imagine the force expended by the player in a Sonata of Beethoven, a Study of Chopin, or a Rhapsody of Liszt! The late Anton Rubinstein says in his interest-pamphlet, entitled " A Conversation on Music,"* " One must have heard Chopin, Liszt, Thalberg, and Henselt to know what genuine piano playing means." Now it is certain that these players, endowed with the finest attributes of tone, and three out of the four masters of the grandest and fullest " forte " tone that has been heard, gained their unrivalled mastery of tone by assiduous practice upon the light German pianos with the so-called Viennese action, compared to which there is in the present day no pianoforte so easy. And this may apply to Rubinstein himself, for even he must have made his early studies upon such instruments.

We have now arrived at a clear comprehension of the leading parts of a modern pianoforte action. There must be the key, hopper, spring and set-off, notch or roller, to raise the hammer while the check comes into service as it falls. The damper is also controlled by the key. According to the mechanism chosen other parts

* Anton Rubinstein, "Die Musik und ihre Meister" (Leipzig: Dritte Auflage, 1892), p. 107. English translation, "A Conversation on Music" (London, 1892), p. 77.

may be present or absent, but these, the principal members, must be there, however placed in position, or whatever proportions they may have, whether the touch is heavy or light, of shallow or deep depression; uninfluenced by the shape of the piano, whether it is grand, upright, or square.

THE STRIKING PLACE.

That division of the string where the hammer strikes is of great importance with respect to tone and its excursion or carrying power,* yet difficult in practice to determine. According to some authorities it should be the eighth of the vibrating length of the string as measured between the bridges—in other words, the node of the eighth partial.† But this seems to be authoritative only for the middle and the lower divisions of the scale; in the upper the striking distance has to come into a ninth, and very much nearer as the scale shortens and the wrest-plank bridge is approached, in order to get a sustained ringing tone. It is a compromise determined by experiment; there is no other way open to the solution of the problem. The seventh is as good a node as the eighth, and the fifth or third node might answer were it not that the string loses support when the striking place is so far away from the wrest-plank bridge; but of these we have no experimental knowledge, the shape of a piano rendering the seventh difficult and the others impossible. The half of the string gives a quality of tone too much like the chalumeau of a clarinet.‡

Helmholtz says: § "In pianofortes the point struck is about $\frac{1}{7}$th to $\frac{1}{9}$th the length of string from its extremity, for the middle part of the instrument. We must therefore assume that this place has been chosen because experience has shown it to give the finest musical tone, which is most suitable for harmonics. The selection is not due to theory. It results from attempts to meet the requirements of artistically trained ears and from the technical experience of two

* The harmonic divisions (nodes) must be aliquot, because vibrations must keep step to continue. A hammer striking between—on a loop—must interfere with the continuity of vibration and disturb the proper sequence of the partials. There are, however, non-harmonic divisions when thickness or width become important, and these are not aliquot. A node is a point of greatest condensation or rarefaction.

† Kütsing, "Theoretisch-practisches Handbuch der Fortepiano-Baukunst" (Bern und Chur, 1844), p. 41.

‡ The Rev. Joseph Cotter produced this tone by exciting the strings at the centre, in a cabinet piano, which he called a Lyrichord, about 1840.

§ Helmholtz, second English edition, 1885, p. 77.

centuries. This gives particular interest to the investigation of the composition of musical tones for this point of excitement. An essential advantage in such a choice of position seems to be that the seventh and ninth partial tones disappear, or at least become very weak. These are the first in the series of partial tones which do not belong to the major chord of the prime tone."

As a commentary upon this passage the late Dr. A. J. Ellis added some observations of mine in a footnote,* which tend to show that a consideration of the best striking-place has not been prominent with pianoforte makers until the present century, and Helmholtz has also overlooked what I have already referred to—the necessary obligation of the harp-like form of the instrument. Dr. Ellis has further† given place to particulars of papers of mine published in the "Proceedings of the Royal Society," Vol. XXXVII., p. 368, and Vol. XXXVIII., p. 83, showing that the harmonic partials adjacent to the striking-place do not invariably disappear. The eighth and ninth are always weak in the piano, but the seventh is strong. I do not question the truth of Young's law, which banishes the partial appertaining to a node used as a striking-place, but I assume that the elasticity of the steel wire recovers itself and may speedily overcome the effect of the hammer-blow by re-establishing the proper harmonic partial tones inherent in the strings.

Helmholtz, and indeed nearly all acousticians, regard the harmonic seventh as a dissonance, and he says it should be rejected from the harmonic chord forming the note. I venture to assert, on the contrary, that this weird consonance and most pathetic note of the Æolian harp should be always there.‡ The minor seventh of our modern harmony, made of two fourths, C—F—B flat, is a dissonance and is of higher pitch than the harmonic seventh. The latter, although existing in trumpets and French horns, is necessarily rejected from our musical system because it is foreign to any notes excepting those in its natural harmonic position, and is, therefore, inimical to modulation. Why it is preferable, as I assume, to find the striking-place upon a node or apparent place of rest in the vibration of the string is because the greater energy is latent in the nodes in which the vibrations

* Helmholtz, second English edition, 1885, p. 77.
† Helmholtz, p. 545.
‡ M. A. Cavaillé-Col, of Par's, demonstrated this necessary inclusion by making a complete harmonic scale of organ pipes to be sounded on one key.

are reduced to an almost infinitesimal amplitude, and in setting this energy free we are adding to the strength and carrying power of the notes. In this way the audible superiority of tone so produced may be accounted for. Experiments with pianos as to the relative strength of the harmonic partials serve to show that the tenth is the highest to be distinctly audible; the eleventh may be heard, but is of uncertain or doubtful perception. This is a trumpet harmonic, too sharp in pitch for the diatonic scale. We may assume that much higher proper tones enter into the composition of the string note, but are too weak to be detected by such methods as we employ; the relative thickness to length of the wire in the treble must also disturb the harmonic relation of the proper tones. The absence of dampers in the treble explains itself by the shortness of the vibration of the treble notes; it would seem, however, to have been also intended to give life and ring to the higher notes of the instrument by leaving this part of the scale free to sympathetic vibration.

THE PEDALS.

In modern pianos, grand or upright, there are two pedals regarded as indispensable, and known as the *piano* and *forte* pedals; some makers add a third, called a tone-sustaining pedal, to give a power of using selected notes undamped. The left foot presses upon the *piano* or soft pedal, which, in grand pianos always, in upright pianos occasionally, shifts the keyboard action bodily, thereby removing the attack of the hammers from three to two strings, and leaving one untouched, but not silent, for it vibrates through the influence of the sounding strings it is in tune with. To this beautiful sympathetic vibration is to be attributed the soft pedal tone quality when so produced, an Æolian charm of which modern composers for the piano, from Chopin and Liszt, have made profit. In many upright pianos, however, although some are made with shifting keyboards, and others to shift the beam or hammer-rail only, a soft pedal is contrived by mechanically dropping a strip of cloth, or thin felt, between the hammers and the strings, making, as it were, a thicker clothing for the hammers, to diminish the amount of tone. This goes by the name of "Celeste." There is another kind of soft pedal now much used, obtained by shortening the radius of the hammer blow, which can only be said to replace the due modifications for *piano* and *pianissimo* of the player's touch.

Some players, who have not given consideration to the nature of the soft pedal, treat it as if its effect could be graduated by putting the pedal down more or less. A moment's reflection should convince anyone thus using a shifting keyboard that there is no halting-place between three strings and two; moreover, when the hammers are shifted, there are indentations or cuts on the surface of the felt caused by the strings, and unless these are directly opposite the strings by a decided shift or return, a snarling quality of tone will be heard, owing to the edges of the cuts on the hammer surface coming into contact with the strings. Up to about 1830 there was a further shift permissible to one string only, the *Una Corda* of Beethoven; its employment was managed by a small hand-stop on one of the key blocks. In those days the hammers were small and of leather, and had much less blow, so that the wear was less than with the large felt hammers and powerful blow of the present day. The surface of the hammers now used would be too much cut up by the practice of a double shift for ordinary service. The right foot or *forte* pedal does away with the use of the dampers throughout. The tone is louder, as all the sympathetic tones the instrument may be able to give forth are called into play. It should not, however, be named the *forte* pedal, as it is not less used in *piano* and *pianissimo* playing. It should be invariably described as the damper pedal; while it is held down by the foot it makes the instrument an undamped one, and its employment allows any note the prerogative by influence of calling forth all higher notes that are in unison with its own partial tones, and the partial tones of all lower notes that happen to agree or be in unison with its own particular note or prime. The player controls all this wealth of sympathetic vibration with the damper pedal, bringing down the dampers upon the strings whenever there is confusion, or any discord displeasing to the ear. A study of the indications given by the best modern composers will show the student the refinement, in controlling such dissonance, the mastership of this pedal brings with it. Used with such knowledge the alternations of an open with a damped instrument tend to excite the imagination, and affect the mood of both player and hearer. The bounds of expression are much extended by the pedals.

The third pedal I have referred to is called a tone-sustaining pedal, and, although not of the Steinways' invention, is met with in their grand pianos. It is a disposition of the damper action whereby the player may prolong any notes or group of notes by putting down this third pedal directly *after* the note or group is struck.

In concluding this simple description of what a pianoforte is and its leading characteristics, my aim is reached if it has led to a better comprehension of a singularly responsive musical instrument, and the promotion of the cultivation of a feeling for tone in all its various gradations, too often disregarded by even technically accomplished pianists. Also to a recognition of the merit and individuality of the pianoforte makers who have attained to eminence, each having worked out for himself the problems here briefly indicated, and produced results stamped by his own personality.

TUNING.

Without going into the subject of how a pianoforte is to be tuned, which would require a separate treatise* and long practice to acquire, a few words may be said in anticipation of questions that may occur to the reader concerning this essential operation; for without the " well tuned piano " neither maker nor player may find profit. The work of the tuner is to turn the wrest-pins up or down, as may be required to get the right tension of the strings forming a note. In modern pianos the pins are put in much tighter than they were formerly, rendering it more difficult to turn them, and to " fine tune " a piano, so as to make each string exactly right according to the judgment of the ear becomes, from the louder and more metallic tone of modern pianos, more and more exacting. It demands considerable power of wrist and very much practice to change the position of the pin by such small movements as are requisite to effect minute changes of pitch, in order to make the groundwork of fourths and fifths, octaves and unisons, true. As the pins, as already said, are tighter, so that persistence

---

* " Dictionary of Music and Musicians "—" Tuning " (A. J. H.), Vol. IV., pp. 187-190; and Hermann Smith, " The Art of Tuning the Pianoforte ' London: Cocks and Co.; New York: Novello, Ewer and Co., 1893.

of forcible playing shall not move them, they require a tuning-key with a long lever handle instead of the old-fashioned T-shaped tuning-hammer. During all this century there have been frequent endeavours to replace the simple wrest-pin, continued from the spinet and harpsichord, by a mechanical contrivance with a screw that a watch key, or one with very little more power, might turn; or by such an arrangement and then a secondary pressure tuning after an approximate pitch has been secured, like the Alibert tuning-pin. By such means tuning would become, it is affirmed, comparatively easy. Of recent years Becker, of St. Petersburg (perhaps experimentally), Brinsmead of London, and Mason and Hamlin, Boston, U.S.A., have been the most prominent advocates of such expedients; but however ingenious and reasonable these inventions may seem they have not come into general use. The professional tuners find them slow of response and tiring to the ear and patience, and the amateur is no nearer to the effective tuning of a piano, inasmuch as hand and ear have still to be trained to go together. The extremes of a pianoforte, both treble and bass, require considerable practice to hear aright, as professional tuners know, and to tune them accurately is yet more difficult. It is an almost certain test of accurate tuning if both ends of the compass, the treble and bass, agree.

The French pitch, or Diapason Normal, is now generally adopted on the Continent and has made its way in the United States of America. In this country, with the exception of the Italian Opera, which has been at the low pitch for the last fifteen years, we may say the high or Philharmonic pitch has, from 1846 to 1895, prevailed. It has been known as Costa's pitch, from its having been the mean pitch of Covent Garden Opera and the Philharmonic Society's Concerts when that distinguished musician was the conductor. He had the same wind instrument players in both orchestras. In 1890 the standard pitch was re-adjusted for Kneller Hall, the training school of musicians for the British Army, it being required by Her Majesty's Rules and Regulations to conform with the Philharmonic pitch. Colonel Shaw Hellier, at that time the Commandant, requested me to determine this standard. As it was required for wind instruments I sought the assistance of Mr. Blaikley, an acoustician and well known expert, and decided upon b^1 flat, 479·3 double vibrations in a second at a temperature of 60° Fahrenheit for the standard fork.

which, in equal temperament, agrees with a' 452·4 and c² 538.* The Philharmonic Society has, however, for 1896, relinquished its high pitch and adopted the Diapason Normal, which Messrs. Novello and Co., as far back as 1869, when establishing the Oratorio Concerts under the conductorship of Sir Joseph (then Mr.) Barnby, made a bold attempt to introduce into this country.† It was, however, premature, and the question of pitch has been allowed to rest with an occasional stir, as at the Opera in 1879, to satisfy Madame Patti, until this measure of the Philharmonic Society has re-introduced it. Setting the military bands aside as forming a province ruled by its own law, the French pitch yet remains as appertaining to preference and not obligation, and will so continue while the great Concert organs of Great Britain are, up to this time with only one exception, at the high pitch. The difference is about two-thirds of an equal semitone; the French pitch being a¹ 870 single or half, 435 double or complete vibrations in a second at 59° Fahrenheit (15° Centigrade).‡ The wind instruments of an orchestra rising in pitch with increase of heat, although not equally, an average rate of increase has to be found to which to tune pianos for public concerts. I regard this rise as equivalent to 1° F. ÷ 1,000, a thousandth part of a vibration or of any number of vibrations in a second for one degree of the Fahrenheit thermometer. This co-efficient is confirmed by observations of wind instruments made under rising temperatures by Mr. Blaikley, § and of the organ by the late Dr. A. J. Ellis.‖ Instead of the normal 59° F. (15° C.), it is advisable for the orchestra and organ to tune to 68° F. (20° C.), an average

* A. J. Ellis, "History of Musical Pitch," p. 329 (London, 1880), and his "Helmholtz," second English edition, p. 502 (London, 1885).

† See *The Musical Times*, No. 312, Vol. XIII., February 1, 1869, pp. 663-5 and 688.

‡ The rate of vibration can be measured accurately by a Scheibler Tonometer of tuning-forks. See "The History of Musical Pitch," by A. J. Ellis, p. 299; Ellis's "Helmholtz," "The Sensations of Tone," second edition, pp. 443, 444; and "Dictionary of Music and Musicians," Scheibler (A. J. H.), Vol. III. (London, 1883), pp. 243, 244.

§ "An Historical Catalogue of the Military Instruments recently exhibited at the Royal Military Exhibition, London, 1890." Compiled by Captain C. R. Day, Oxfordshire Light Infantry. Appendix: an "Essay on Musical Pitch," by D. J. Blaikley, p. 247. Eyre and Spottiswoode, London, 1891. Mr. Blaikley's co-efficient for the organ practically agrees with Dr. A. J. Ellis's and my own.

‖ Proceedings of the Royal Society, No. 205, 1880. "Notes of Observations on Musical Beats," by Alexander J. Ellis; p. 5 of Reprint.

concert temperature. The piano will then have to be adjusted to a^1 439 = c^2 522 equal temperament.* The temperature of the organ in the flue pipes, under increase of heat, scarcely differs from that of free air. The larger brass instruments approach it; the wood-wind is more affected by the warmth of the player's breath, particularly in winter. The flattening of the fork under increase of temperature is so small, no more than 1° F. ÷ 20,000, that I follow Ellis in disregarding it, and I also disregard any possible fall in the pitch of the piano as the temperature rises, because I believe, for the time the instrument is required, the elasticity of the cast steel wire is a sufficient counter-action.

Fairly accurate tuning-forks can easily be acquired for either pitch; C forks being in more general use in this country, the French one should be 517·3. If forks are within ·5, or half a vibration a second, they are near enough for use. The keyboard instruments are necessarily tuned in semitones of equal width or equal temperament, the groundwork for which is obtained by very slightly flattening ascending fifths or descending fourths, the major thirds and sixths being all equally and considerably sharp upwards. This manner of tuning approaches the Greek tuning of Pythagoras, and is very near the Hemitonal division of Aristoxenus; it has been generally used in this country for pianos nearly fifty years. Before then the tuning was unequal, intended to be mean tone temperament, which left some keys almost unplayable to benefit those with fewer sharps and flats. Equal temperament has its drawbacks, but it is impossible to play on keyboard instruments in all keys, or chromatic music, by any other system. It has the high authority of John Sebastian Bach, as shown in the Forty-eight Preludes and Fugues ("Das Wohltemperirte Clavier," the well-tuned Clavichord or Harpsichord). A good tuner can come very near the theoretical division of this temperament, near enough for practical purposes.

It should be remembered that mathematical statements of tuning, often carried to several places of decimals, only exist on paper. The average musical ear does not distinguish smaller differences than ·2, a fifth of a complete vibration a second, in any part of the scale, more often ·3 or a third; and in musical problems the ear alone is the arbiter without appeal to intellectual subtleties.

* See "Musical Pitch." Journal of the Society of Arts, Feb. 28, 1896, p. 342. March 24, 1897, the Philharmonic Society publicly announced the adoption of this vibration number and temperature as the Standard Philharmonic Pitch. It so happens 439 is the exact mean between the lowest Philharmonic Pitch, Peppercorn 1813, A = 423.3, and the highest recorded by me in July, 1874, A = 454.7.

Part 2.

HISTORICAL.

KEYBOARD STRINGED INSTRUMENTS
Which Preceded the Pianoforte to a.d. 1800.

THE KEYBOARD.

As the various keyboard instruments have in common the apparatus of levers and touch keys for eliciting the sound, it is desirable to begin an historical division with a consideration of its origin and of some peculiarities that have at certain times affected its construction and use. Such a study might have found place in the description of one or other of the older instruments of the keyboard class, but as this could not be done without cross references a general statement is preferable.

Although the organ and instruments of the organ kind, as the old regal and modern harmonium, are not included in my subject, it is yet impossible to deal with the keyboard without some reference to the organ in its historical connection; and the first invented of the keyboard instruments having been the organ, the origin of the keyboard must be sought for in connection with that instrument. It does not matter whether it had at first a set of slides, analogous to draw-stops, or a set of balanced levers, the idea is the mechanical one of a succession of keys to open sound, and I am indebted to Mr. Warman, the author of an interesting work upon the organ,* for pointing out to me that Vitruvius, in the first century a.d.,†

---

* John W. Warman, "The Organ: its compass, tablature, and short and incomplete octaves." London: William Reeves, 1884.

† "Vitruvius, de Architectura," Lib. X., cap. xi., translated by Newton. See "The Organ: its History and Construction," E. J. Hopkins and E. F. Rimbault, LL.D. (London: Cocks & Co., 1870), pp. 6, 7, 8, in which, however, the description of the key apparatus is not observed; also "The Pneumatics of Hero of

described a balanced keyboard. The hydraulic organ was invented by Ctesibius, of Alexandria, in the second century B.C., and may have had keys in the acceptation I have just defined for unlocking sound. Unfortunately the early representations of this instrument, which occur on Roman coins, show the pipes from the back, leaving us in doubt as to the exact form and manipulation of the key mechanism. Bottée de Toulmon, in an engraving which accompanies a lecture read by him upon a monument at Constantinople of the time of Theodosius,* depicts a prize awarder standing with floral crown in hand and attendants; on a lower plane, and smaller in size, are dancers moving to the music of three sets of double pipes and two pneumatic organs—one with seven, the other with eight pipes. Two men stand on the bellows of each to keep them going, but the backs of the organs are towards the spectator.† However, the descriptions in Newton's version of the Hydraulicon of Vitruvius, and also the Pneumatics of Hero, may be regarded as settling the question of balanced keys acting by cranks directly connected with the slides and returned to their equilibrium by springs of horn. But handle slides may have also been used and probably were, as shown in a drawing reproduced by Rimbault‡ from an old manuscript attributed to the time of Charlemagne.

The application of keys to stop (shorten) strings was first attempted with instruments of the hurdy-gurdy class; still the Monochord, the interval measurer and pitch carrier, was hand-stopped by means of little bridges up to the time of Guido d'Arezzo, who is said to have been born about A.D. 995, and later. The adaptation of a keyboard to a polychord stringed instrument was long attributed to Guido, but the credit of this important invention has, of late years, been withdrawn from him. When in the thirteenth century, perhaps in the twelfth, the small "Portative"

Alexandria," translated from the original Greek by Bennett Woodcroft (London, 1851), in which the key movement is more particularly described and figured; copied in Hopkins and Rimbault, p. 157, and Hauser, "Geschichte des Christlichen, insbesondere des kirchlichen Evangelien Gesanges und der Kirchenmusik" (Quedlinburg, 1834), p. 13, where a water-organ is also figured.

* Bottée de Toulmon, "Mémoires de la Société Royale des Antiquaires de France," Nouvelle Série, Tome XVII., Paris, 1840. "Dissertation sur les instruments de musique employés au Moyen-âge," p. 127, Planche IV., circa A.D. 400.

† The organ is figured in Hopkins and Rimbault, p. 16.

‡ Hopkins and Rimbault, "The Organ," p. 30.

organ came into use—by Fétis, Rimbault, and Engel called "Regal" —furnished with narrow keys (in many instances mere finger-stops shaped like gimlets), the dawn of the string keyboard was near. Don Juan Riaño* gives a drawing copied from the "Cantigas de Santa Maria," an authenticated Spanish manuscript of the thirteenth century, in which a portative organ (*portatif*) with nine pipes and ordinary keys appears; the keys in two rows and, we may infer, five below the player's thumb, which hides one; and also one copied from a fresco in the Cistercian Monastery of Neustra Señora de Piedra, Aragon, the date of which is 1390. Here are three rows of pipes and balanced white natural keys, with a square additional key inserted of the same level, not a raised key. Assuming† the instrument to end upwards with a^1, following Greek precedent, this inserted key would be b flat, a note required for transposition. Guido's scale had two b flats, and Virdung,‡ in 1511, figures such a keyboard, which he attributes to a clavichord; but his drawing is of a pattern too near his own time to be relied upon without other evidence. To a certain extent early paintings supply illustration of the keyboards of portative organs. For example, we find in a picture by Fra Angelico,§ in the National Gallery, an instance of inserted accidental keys in a portative organ, suggestive of cadences; but the indications are obscure unless seen under strong light. In large organs the full chromatic scale even then existed, as in the Halberstadt organ, which, according to an inscription, was built in A.D. 1361 and restored A.D. 1495, and had, I believe from the earlier date, this semitonal arrangement of keys. The compass of the keyboards coincided with a Greek tetrachordal scale, from B natural in the bass clef (Hypate Hypaton) to a^1 in the treble clef (Nete Hyperbolæon), and this confirms me in the certainty of the

* Don Juan Riaño, "Notes on Early Spanish Music" (Quaritch, London, 1887), pp. 119-127.
† "Cantor Lectures on Musical Instruments," by A. J. Hipkins, F.S.A. Society of Arts, London, 1891, p. 764; of reprint, 22.
‡ Sebastian Virdung, "Musica getutscht und auszgezogen." Basle, 1511 (*Fac-simile* reprint, Berlin, 1882. "Gesellschaft für Musikforschung." Edited by Robert Eitner).
§ Catalogue of the Pictures in the National Gallery (London, 1889), No 663; and "The Hobby Horse," 1893, No. 1. "The Musical Instruments of the Angels, represented in early Italian paintings in the National Gallery," by A. J. Hipkins, p. 15.

keyboard of the organ, and afterwards of the spinet, having followed the Greek system of music as followed in the Schools. From Prætorius* we learn the gradual extension of the compass, from St. Aegidius at Brunswick and the Halberstadt organs until, in A.D. 1493, the great organ at Bamberg, which had, when first built eighteen years before, started from B natural, but in that year was completed with a compass of three octaves and a third from F below the bass clef to a^2 above the treble,† the lowest F being carried down in long measure (not short octave), rejecting the lowest F sharp and G sharp. The F had gained its place from the "molle" hexachord of Guido, the diatonic series of six notes which included B flat, and it stood as the lowest note of the deep or bass voice. As the large or church organ keyboard was extended the width of its keys was lessened, so that from the grasp of a fifth the player's stretch could at last include an octave. In 1499 the octave of the great organ of St. Blaise, at Brunswick, required a stretch of nine keys only of the keyboard of Prætorius's time. The early keyboard of the clavicymbal, virginal or spinet, followed the portative and positive organs in narrow keys, and with the Greek tetrachordal arrangement from E of the middle (meson) or B of the lower (hypaton) tetrachord; and we find this in nearly all sixteenth century instruments, but an octave lower in pitch; an extension spoken of by Virdung,‡ and as convenient for pedals. When the Halberstadt organ was built, the lowest tetrachord, starting from B̲, was still untouched by the drone or short octave device, as is shown by the measure, given by Prætorius, of the lowest pipe;§ but subsequent to this date, and certainly by the beginning of the sixteenth century, a different ordering of the pipes, or in spinets of the stringing, was introduced to accommodate the old harmony, as it is called in Prætorius, of a drone (the modern "point d'orgue"), which served as a foundation for the melody, and the counterpoint woven round it. To provide the drone notes the lowest octave was tuned in a short measure, the width of a sixth only,

---

* Michael Prætorius, "Syntagmatis Musici, Tomus Secundus De Organographia" (Wolfenbüttel, 1618), p. 111; reprint, p. 134; et "Theatrum Instrumentorum seu Sciagraphia," 1620.

† Cantor Lectures, A. J. Hipkins, p. 766; reprint, p. 24.

‡ Virdung, F.

§ Prætorius, p. 101; reprint, p. 122; and see A. J. Ellis's "History of Musical Pitch," *Journal of the Society of Arts*, March 5, 1880; and reprint, p. 332

and known as a short octave, the "*mi, re, ut*" of Diruta,* by which the bass, beginning apparently with E, sounded C; F sharp, D; and G sharp, E; in descending order *mi, re, ut*. Or if the lowest note was B, then the drone or pedal note that was upon that key sounded G; C sharp, A; and the D sharp, B natural; unless the D sharp was left to serve for E flat—for transposition a more valuable note.

There have been other short octave arrangements to attain the same end,† but these given were the normal for the sixteenth and seventeenth centuries. The sound-board bridge of the spinet was not altered in the curve to meet the irregular scaling demanded by the short octave, it was effected easily by putting on strings of increased thickness for the deeper notes. If there were any doubt about the short octave, Diruta, Prætorius,‡ Mersenne,§ and other contemporary writers are corroborated by existing specimens of the instruments which have the keys so lettered. When the chromatic scale became a recognised system, and practicable, by more equal tuning of the semitones—that is to say, in the seventeenth and early years of the eighteenth century—the lowest sharps or raised keys were often broken or divided, by making distinct keys and notes of the separated halves, reserving the back half for the semitone and continuing the lower drone note upon the front half, so that the chromatic, and *mi, re, ut*, or short octave notes, were both available,|| thus :—

$$F\sharp, G\sharp,$$
$$D, E, B\flat,$$
$$C, F, G, A, B\natural, C.$$

* Diruta, " Transilvano Dialogo sopra il vere mododi sonar Organi ed instromenti di penna. Del R. P. Girolamo Diruta Perugino. Dell Ordine de' Frati Minori Conu, di S. Francesco . . . In Venetia, Appresso Giacomo Vincenti, MDXCVII." See E. Dannreuther, " Musical Ornamentation," Part I.— " Girolamo Diruta," Novello, 1891 ; and Carl Krebs, " Girolamo Diruta's Transilvano." " Ein Beitrag zur Geschichte des Orgel- und Klavierspiels im 16 Jahrhundert." Breitkopf and Härtel, Leipzig, 1892.

† Ammerbach, "Elias Nicolaus, Orgel oder Instrument Tabulatur." Leipzig, 1571. Mr. Taphouse, of Oxford, has played upon an organ of Father Smith's, which followed Ammerbach's arrangement thus :   C   D   B♭
                                                         E F   G   A   B♮ C.

‡ Prætorius, p. 187 ; reprint, 219.

§ Mersenne, " F. Marin, de l'ordre de Minimes, Harmonie Universelle " (Paris, 1636), Liv. III., p. 107.

|| Prætorius, p. 202 ; reprint, p. 234.

the scale continuing simply chromatic afterwards. The late Carl Engel* mistook these divided sharps for quarter-tones, although he did not attempt to explain the use such small intervals could be put to, and especially at so grave a pitch. And Dr. Carl Krebs,† a recent German writer upon keyboard instruments, has been similarly misled. In point of fact, the scale of a clavichord with divided sharps in the Berlin Instrumental Museum, which Dr. Krebs attributes to the early part of the sixteenth century, may be shown by this peculiarity to belong to a much later date. And allowing that the instrument may, from its style of case, be attributable to the earlier period, the present scaling and key division may have been the work of a later restorer, as the confused state of the tangents suggests. One string only to a note is not a sufficient warrant for fixing an early date. There were three string clavichords at the beginning of the sixteenth century, as Virdung tells us,‡ and those with one string only to a note were not impossible at a later date.

While the spinet followed the organ closely in the disposition of the keyboard, the clavichord, so far as we have early examples or descriptions, adhered to the hexachordal conception of Guido, as developed from the division of the monochord. The lowest bass notes starting from F or C—but A in some instances occurred—not G, as from the "durum" hexachord, might have been expected. Short, and mixed or broken octaves, sometimes however happen, as in the clavichord the possession of which is traditionally attributed to Handel. There is another long measure, as already mentioned, occasionally to be met with, proceeding from F, G, A to B flat, and so on chromatically. Boxwood appears to have preceded ivory as the material for the natural or lower touch keys (a Regal in my possession, the only large one in this country, has spotted or bird's eye maple), the sharps or upper keys were ebony, or stained dark. In elaborate instruments tortoiseshell and mother-of-pearl, and even costly inlays were not infrequent.

* Carl Engel, "A Descriptive Catalogue of the Musical Instruments in the South Kensington Museum," second edition (London, 1874), p. 351.

† Carl Krebs, "Die besaiteten Klavier Instrumente bis zum Anfang des 17 Jahrhunderts." Berlin, Separatabdruck aus der Vierteljahrschrift fur Mus. Wissenschaft, 1892, p. 100.

‡ Virdung, F.

The recently introduced Janko keyboard* has as yet made too little way to justify me to dwell upon it here. There are mechanical objections that must impede its acceptance with pianists. It is the latest of a long series of experiments to obtain what are sometimes called symmetrical keyboards, for which one or two fingerings for all scales suffice, in contradistinction to the normal division of the upper keys, by two and three alternately, due to the relative position of the intervals of the fourth and fifth in the octave, and requiring several fingerings.†

THE UNDETERMINED MUSICAL INSTRUMENTS.

Echiquier (Exaquir)—Eschaqueil d'Angleterre, Dulce Melos, Symphonia.

The Echiquier as a musical instrument occurs in French poetry of the fourteenth century :—

> Fors plantiau le musicien
> Qui je ne quant je l'en requier,
> De la Harpe et d'eschiquier.
>
> Je n'aie si mal en l'ongle
> Que je n'aie appris à jouer
> A l'eschiquier et flajolet.
>
> Eustache Deschamps.

also in a fifteenth century poem by Molinet, entitled, "Chanson sur la journée de Guingate" :—

> Orgues, harpes, naquaires, challemelles,
> Bons échiquiers, guisternes, doucemelles;

and there are other instances.

The Echiquier had eluded classification as a musical instrument until Mr. Edmond Vander Straeten,‡ while searching for evidence

---

* Janko, Paul von, "Eine Neue Claviatur." Vienna, 1886.

† "Dictionary of Music and Musicians"—"Key" or "Keyboard" (A. J. H.) Vol. II., pp. 54, 55; and Vol. IV., p. 690, where there is a brief description of the Janko keyboard and the advantages claimed for it. The idea of reducing scale fingerings, say, to two for all keys, is not of recent origin, nor of reducing the stretch of the hand upon the keyboard so that an octave can be grasped in the usual width of a fifth or sixth. C. Hänfling in 1708, and again in 1710, propounded such an invention with a full description and engravings. A paragraph in Adlung's "Musica Mechanica Organaedi," II., 131, is devoted to it.

‡ Edmond Vander Straeten, "La Musique aux Pays-Bas avant le XIX^a Siècle," tome septième, p. 40. Brussels, 1885.

of a Flemish influence upon music in Spain, came upon a Spanish form of this name "Exaquir." It was a stringed instrument furnished with a keyboard, but whether acted upon by a stop or fretting contrivance like the simple tangent of the clavichord, by plectra like a spinet or harpsichord, or on a principle not now known to us, we cannot say. A possible synonymous "L'eschaqueil" occurs in "La Prise d'Alexandrie," and "L'eschaqueil d'Angleterre," in "Li temps pastour," a fourteenth century poem by Guillaume de Machault,* suggests an English origin for the instrument. Dr. Carl Krebs says:† "It is remarkable that Guillaume de Machault has written 'Eschaqueil d'Angleterre.' England may have been the home of this instrument, and as Exaquir comes nearest to the English form Exchequer . . . we may suppose that it was introduced into Spain from thence, and probably by the roundabout way of the Netherlands. . . . Perhaps the stringed keyboard instruments were not first built in Italy, as is usually accepted; it will be interesting, should subsequent research succeed in connecting the Eschaqueil d'Angleterre with the fact, that in England Virginal music had already fully bloomed, when elsewhere the stringed clavier had only begun to assume independence of the organ."

Mr. Vander Straeten's discovery tells us that in 1387, King John of Aragon requested his brother-in-law, Philip the Hardy, Duke of Burgundy, to send him an Exaquir, and in 1388, in repeating this request, the King described it as "semblant d'orguens qui sona ab cordes" (resembling an organ which sounds with strings). This might mean what is called a claviorganum, a spinet or harpsichord with a small organ attached, playable with the same keyboard; and Dr. Krebs came across such an "espinette organisée" in the great Music Exhibition which took place at Vienna in 1892,‡ that, closing up like a draughtboard, the name of exaquir, échiquier or exchequer, might have been appropriate to. The word undoubtedly means a chess or draughtboard, inasmuch as a literal German rendering occurs in Eberhard

* Bibliothèque Nationale, Paris: "La Prise d'Alexandrie," MS., No. 25; "Li Temps Pastour," MS., No. 7,221.

† Carl Krebs, "Die besaiteten Klavier Instrumente," pp. 94, 95.

‡ E. Vander Straeten, "La Fédération Artistique," No. 27, April 23, 1893, p. 316. "Toujours l'échiquier musical."

Cersne of Minden's rules of the Minnesingers, dated 1404, and preserved in the Hofbibliothek, Vienna,* where we find: "Schachtbret (modern Schachbrett, derived from schachten, to square), Monocordium," "Rotte, Clavicordium," "Lûte, Clavicimbolum." I have elsewhere suggested† that the name may have come from the decoration of the case; the black and white chequers occurring on a portative organ in an altar-piece by Orcagna.‡ Dr. Krebs, quoting from Ducange, gives an analogous word, "scararium," at first a chessboard and then a table whereon a chessboard stood; the old Exchequer Court of Law in London has been supposed to derive its name from the room in which it was held having a chequered floor.

The Doucemelle already named with the Echiquier in the "Chanson sur la journée de Guingate," is a French form of the Latin Dulce Melos which, although usually the common dulcimer, upon the authority of an anonymous manuscript§ in the Paris Library, attributed to the fifteenth century, had also a keyboard variety. This manuscript was brought to light by Bottée de Toulmon, in a lecture read by him before the French Society of Antiquaries, in Paris, 1840, and published in its Proceedings.|| Fétis subsequently described the manuscript¶ as chiefly concerned with astronomical instruments, but containing a treatise, "De compositione clavicembali (the clavicembalo being the spinet or virginal, and later the harpsichord), clavicordi, &c.," and another, "De Organis." Bottée de Toulmon went so far as to believe he had come upon a very early pianoforte, and he says in his lecture: "The Dulce Melos was a piano. One would never have thought that a piano could have existed in the fifteenth century; however, there is no doubting it. The author gives a drawing and a description of the *dulce melos*. It is a piano of *four* octaves. He says at the beginning that this instrument can be made in three ways; unfortunately he only indicates two." It is the second that has the keyboard, and further

---

* Ambros, "Geschichte der Musik," First edition, Vol. II., p. 507.

† "Cantor Lectures on Musical Instruments," by A. J. Hipkins. *Journal of the Society of Arts*, August 14, 1891, p. 770; reprint, p. 28.

‡ Catalogue of the Pictures in the National Gallery (London, 1889), No. 569.

§ Bibliotèque Nationale de Paris (Krebs, No. 1,118; Fétis, No. 7,295).

|| "Dissertation sur les instruments de musique employés au Moyen-âge," p. 64.

¶ "Histoire générale de la Musique depuis les temps les plus anciens jusqu'à nos jours" (Paris, 1874), Vol. V., p. 201.

on Bottée says the compass is chromatic, from B natural (apparently in the bass stave) to a^2, corresponding with the fourteenth century Halberstadt organ, which was also chromatic but ranging an octave lower. The compass in the fifteenth century was being added to gradually. The manuscript really gives the clavichord three octaves while to the "clavicembalum" the compass of the *dulce melos* only— viz., three octaves, less a whole tone. Fétis gives a different scale for the "clavicin"—*i.e.*, "clavicembalum"—viz., three octaves and a third, D—f^2, 40 keys; but says some were F—g^2, 39 keys. Bottée's four octaves appears to have been a mistake. Fétis regards the *dulce melos* as more rational than the clavichord, having as many strings as notes, and the sounds as less sharp, being struck with light pieces of wood instead of blades of metal. According to Bottée, the manuscript allows single or double strings, to the *dulce melos* as well as to the clavicordium and clavicembalum.

The Symphonia is another undetermined keyboard instrument, although named by Schlick* and Prætorius.† Not one, however, of these writers describes what is meant by this name. Schlick says: "No organ work or positive, whatsoever pipes they may have, of metal, wood, paper, linen or glass, and the same of musical instruments with metal or gut strings, as 'clavicordia,' 'clavizymmell,' 'symphonien,' lutes, harps, and others. . ." It will be observed that he separates the symphonia from the clavichord and clavicymbal. Cocleus,‡ in a Latin text, speaks of the "clavichordium" with brass and iron wires touched by keys, and if the instrument is softer the instrument is called "symphonia," if louder "clavicymbalum," indicating gradations in power, but how achieved is not explained. Lastly, Prætorius says,§ "Thus the clavichordium is the fundamental of all keyboard instruments, such as the organs, clavicymbels, symphonies, spinets, virginals, &c., and therefore organ pupils should from the beginning be instructed upon it." A complete list, but still separating the symphonia.

* Schlick, Arnold, "Spiegel der Orgelmacher und Organisten" (? Mainz, 1511). Reprint in the "Monatshefte fur Musik-Geschichte von der Gesellschaft fur Musikforschung." Erste Jahrgang, 1869 ; Redigirt von Robert Eitner (Berlin), p. 101.

† Prætorius, pp. 61, 62 ; reprint, pp. 72, 73.

‡ Krebs, p. 112. He quotes from Cocleus. ("Tetrachordum Musices," Nuremberg, 1512, cap. 9.)

§ Prætorius, p. 61 ; reprint, p. 72.

Heading the next chapter Symphonia, he says: "A 'symphony' (as also a clavicymbalum, virginale, spinetta) is, commonly with the most of the others, named indifferently 'instrument'; but this is too general as it comprises all musical instruments, . . . it should not be restricted to kind, and specially attached or referred to symphonies and clavicymbels." Then he speaks of* "how you require a symphonia, clavicymbel, and the like instruments strung and quilled," thus excluding the clavichord, which is not quilled. Dr Carl Krebs sees in the symphonia a clavichord with one string to a note, which may be the solution, supposing that it was a slip of Prætorius to speak of quilling. Or it may have been another and later name for the keyboard *dulce melos*, the tone of which, with light wooden tangents, would be extremely soft. We have not yet succeeded in finding out what the Echiquier (Eschaqueil d'Angleterre), *dulce melos* as a keyboard instrument, and Symphonia, really were.

CLAVICHORD.

The clavichord, especially in the earlier models, shows its descent from the monochord, or pitch carrier with one string. Virdung,† as long ago as 1511, said he never could learn who, by putting keys to a monochord, had invented the clavichord, or who, on account of those keys, first gave the name "clavicordium."
Pythagoras measured a vibrating string stretched between raised bridges on a resonance box, and by shifting those bridges he was enabled to accurately determine the intervals of the Greek diatonic scale. It has been supposed Pythagoras found the monochord in Egypt, where the principle of the stopped string upon a finger-board had been known, as the monuments testify, ages before his time, and it may have been also known in Babylonia. After Pythagoras the monochord became in Greece, where polychord instruments had prevailed, and in Europe generally, the canon or rule for the measurement of intervals, and continued to be so employed up to the eleventh century and later of our era. It became subsequently transformed into a polychord with four strings, to facilitate the melodic division of

---

* Prætorius, p. 150 (pp. 177, 178 of the reprint).
† Virdung, "Musica getutscht," E., ii.

the Gregorian tones, the Plain-song of the Church as used in the Ritual. Such an instrument would be a set of monochords, and in course of time, by adding more strings and a keyboard, the clavichord was invented. We do not know within a hundred years or more when this change happened, but the clavichord, being a development of the monochord, long bore the same name—indeed, up to the end of the sixteenth century. In Dr. Murray's Oxford Dictionary[*] we find, A.D. 1598, *Florio*, "Monocordo, an instrument having manie strings of one sound, which with little peeces of cloth make distinct sounds, called clarichords." Florio evidently confusing damping with the stopping contrivance.

The name in an early form, "Clavicordium," occurs with "Monocordium," "Clavicymbolum" and "Schachtbrett" (see Echiquier) in some old German rules of the Minnesingers, dated 1404. It is the earliest instance of these names.[†] As already said, monochord and clavichord were for a long while interchangeable terms; apart from the clavichord, monochord is understood to mean the large bowed Tromba Marina. In the Latin countries Manicordo (Italian), Manicordio (Spanish), and Manicorde (French) was always a clavichord, while Clavicordo (Italian), Clavicordio (Spanish), and Clavicorde (French) implied a spinet. In an inventory found in Spain by Mr. Edmond Vander Straeten, dated 1480, a clavichord with tangents appears under the name of Manicordio. This transposition of names in England, Holland, or Germany is less noticeable, if it occurred at all. English examples from Dr. Murray's Oxford Dictionary are: *Clavichord*, A.D. 1483, Caxton, *G. de la Tour*, K. vi.: "Where his vyell and clavicordes were." A.D. 1502, Privy purse expenses, Elizabeth of York (published 1830), 41: "A straungier that gave the Quene a payre of clavycordes." Pair, although applied to a single instrument, means something divided into measurable degrees, as in the locution "a pair of stairs." Pair of clavichords, of virginals, of organs, or regals was of frequent occurrence. Then as to clarichord—a corruption that perhaps happened in copying by substituting an "r" for a "v," and afterwards became common; although Dr. Murray mentions the alternative of the Latin *clarus* (clear), instead of *clavis* (key).

---

[*] James A. H. Murray, L.L.D., "A New English Dictionary on Historical Principles" (Oxford, 1889).

[†] Ambros, Vol. II., pp. 167, 210, 507.

A.D. 1508, the will of Wyldegrys (Somerset House), "Payre of Clarycordes." A.D. 1509, *Hawes Past Pleas*, XVI., XII.: "Rebeckes, Clarycordes, eche in theyr degre." A.D. 1514, *Test Ebor.* (Surtees), V. 49: "My best claricordis." It is not quite certain whether clavichords with tangents are intended in these quotations, or spinets. Again, from the wall proverbs at Leckington in Yorkshire, now destroyed, the quotation from a copy in the British Museum, *temp.* Henry VII.:—

> He that fingerithe well the Claricordis maketh a good songe,
> For in the meane (middle part) is the melody with a rest longe,
> If the tewnys be not pleasant to him that hath no skyll,
> Yet no lac to the claricorde for he doith his goode will,
> He that covytithe in clarisymbalis to make good concordance,
> Ought to finger the keys with discrete temperaunce.*

Clarisymbal and claricorde are clearly separated.

The oldest book treating upon musical instruments is Sebastian Virdung's "Musica getutscht und auszgezogen," already quoted from, published in the German language and in the form of a dialogue, with woodcuts, at Basle, in 1511. He describes and figures the clavichord.† His woodcuts of keyboard instruments should be reversed,‡ the keyboards being wrong as to the position of bass and treble. They have been copied by other writers as incorrectly printed in Virdung's book, and the fault was not observed even by those who immediately followed him—Martin Agricola,§ for example, and Luscinius;|| even in these later days Dr. Rimbault¶ continued the error without explaining if he saw it. Fétis, however, noticed it and attributed it to the draughtsmen; but excepting in one instance, an evident blunder, it was due to the drawings not having been reversed for the engraver. The oldest dated clavichord, on the tangent principle, known to me is of Italian origin, and is of the trapeze form like a spinet. It is inscribed A.D. 1547, and was shown in the Historical Collection of

---

* E. F. Rimbault, "The Pianoforte: its origin, progress, and construction" (London, 1860), p. 44.

† Virdung, B. E. F.

‡ See Art. "Pianoforte," "Encyclopædia Britannica," A. J. H. A. & C. Black, 1885.

§ Martin Agricola, " Musica Instrumentalis." Wittenberg, 1529.

|| Luscinius, " Musurgia sive Praxis Musici." Strasburg, 1536.

¶ Rimbault, "The Pianoforte," p. 30.

the Paris Exhibition, 1889, by M. Thibout *fils*. There may, however, be older undated. This clavichord bears the name Dominicus Pisaurensis.* It has four octaves, F to f^3, approximately Virdung's compass. The natural keys are of citron wood and the sharps of ebony. It is, of course, "gebunden" or fretted. The damper is a narrow band of soft stuff attached with glue to the hitch-pin block (opposite to the wrest-pin block). It has a curved, or spinet belly-bridge. As the early clavichords were strung with wire in equal lengths, the instrument was long regarded as a set of monochords. The scaling was effected by the line of the tangents attached to the keys on the left hand side of the player, the sound-board bridges (at that time three or more) resting upon the narrow belly on the right hand side. The belly never covered the keys.

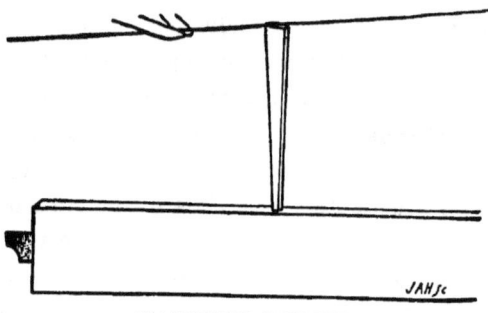

CLAVICHORD TANGENT.

The strings were of brass, sometimes, in the treble, of steel or iron; but brass was preferred for the tone. Owing to the length of the scale large clavichords cannot be tuned high. The tangents are simply upright blades of brass, slender stoppers as shown in the accompanying diagram, fastened into the keys and beaten out at the top, so as to touch equally the one string or the two or three unison strings forming a note. A tangent was thus a bridge or *capo tasto* and a sound exciter. Then by a twisted direction of the keys, each of these little groups of strings or, in rare instances, single string—excepting perhaps some of the lowest and highest in the scale—was acted

* There is a harpsichord existing inscribed "Domenica da Pesaro, 1590." It has two registers, spinet and octave, and stops for them at the side. One keyboard, compass E—f^3, with short octave; boxwood keys; slips of ivory let into the black sharps. Leather plectra, probably original, but this cannot be affirmed. And another, inscribed with the same name, dated as early as 1533, is in the Kraus Museum, Florence. *Vide* Catalogue, p. 15.

upon by two or sometimes three or four tangents to obtain as many notes, so that there were more keys and tangents than string notes. There were no front key-pins to obviate lateral movement; this was checked by little strips of whalebone fastened into the back ends of the keys and confined by a grooved rack at the hitch-pin block. The damping was contrived with a list of cloth, also shown in the diagram, interwoven among the strings, behind the line of the tangents; or occasionally in small instruments a cloth strip laid upon them to form a complete sourdine or mute. The tangent coming in contact with the strings, so long as the key is pressed down, sets them in vibration from the point of impact to the belly-bridge; and when the key is released by the finger, it quits the strings, and the cloth instantly damps them—that is to say, stops their vibration, making them silent. The clavichord is the only keyboard instrument that is amenable to the Vibrato—or Bebung, as the Germans have called this kind of touch; and the Portamento or sharpened pitch by touch pressure.* The divided bridges on the belly lasted in practice as late as 1659, as is shown in an Italian clavichord in the Kraus Museum at Florence; the curved spinet bridge had however been introduced long before with the harp-shaped scale of stringing, replacing entirely the old monochord scale of equal length and divided bridges. In the later large clavichords the lowest notes had overstrung octave strings.

Clavichords with pedals are mentioned by Virdung† and by Reynvaan,‡ the author of a valuable musical dictionary in the Dutch language that was left uncompleted. They are also particularly described by Adlung.§ From these authorities we learn that some clavichords had two octaves and a note of pedals attached to a separate clavichord pedalier, and "fretted," there being three strings in the lower, four in the upper range for each pedal note. Herr Paul de Wit, of Leipzig, has the good fortune to possess a double (two keyboards) clavichord with a separate pedal board. It is a combination of three instruments. The lower manual one can be

* Bach, C. P. E., Versuch; Berlin, 1753, pp. 126-7. Exempel, Tab. VI., Fig. IV., IVA.
† Virdung, F.
‡ Reynvaan, J. Verschuere, "Musijkaal Kunst Woordenboek," Amsterdam, MDCCXCV. In this scarce book the clavichord receives much attention.
§ Adlung, Jakob, "Musica Mechanica Organoedi" (Berlin, 1768), Vol. II., pp. 158-9.

drawn forward when required for performance. The pedalier is, of course, lowest in position, of eight and sixteen-foot strings overspun, the keyboard instruments being of four-foot pitch. There are twenty-five pedals. The maker's inscription is "Johann David Gerstenberg, Orgelbauer zu Geringswald, hat uns gemacht, 1760."*

Ultimately the double stopping became the normal, and the open notes produced by the farthest tangents backwards were F, G, A, B flat, C, D, E flat, the seventh Gregorian tone transposed, and a possible heritage from the old transposition scales (the Heptas) of the Greeks.† In this arrangement the D and A were free, or single tangent notes, without other stopping on those strings, the other strings having a double stopping in order to obtain the notes required to complete the chromatic scale. To do this F sharp was fretted upon F, shortening the strings by so much as is required to make the semitone; G sharp upon G, B natural upon B flat, C sharp upon C, and E natural upon E flat. The choice of the scale notes so as to leave A and D free depended upon the tuning, thus: the tuner would take four fifths up, F—C, C—G, G—D, D—A (tuning down the G an octave to bring the notes conveniently near), and two fifths down or fourths up, F—B flat—E flat; thus securing the seven notes in a diatonic system without the leading semitone. Then the scale was made chromatic by stopping or fretting with additional tangents as already described. The tuner might have taken six upward fifths so as to get E and B natural open, and this was, it is said, in the eighteenth century done;‡ but a groundwork with this intention was not thought of when the Church Modes prevailed. The A and D were prominent notes in the first and second modes, and the B flat and E flat had more importance, especially the B flat, as notes of transposition than the corresponding natural notes.

Other scalings in the old clavichords appear to have been arbitrary. For instance, a threefold stopping, of which the open or single tangent notes in the octave were F, G sharp, B natural, and D. In this scale, F, F sharp, and G are upon one pair or triplet of unison strings; G sharp, A, and A sharp on the next in order of succession; B, C, and C sharp on the next; D, D sharp,

---

* "Zeitschrift für Instrumentenbau" (Leipzig, 1894), pp. 649, 650.

† R. Westphal, "Aristoxenus von Tarent, Melik und Rhythmik des Classischen Hellenthums" (Leipzig, 1883), p. 429.

‡ Jacob Adlung, "Musica Mechanica Organoedi" (Berlin, 1768), p. 148.

and E on the next, and so on.* These artifices for double and treble stopping, survivals from the monochord, were, in Germany, classed as "gebunden," meaning fretted, a term adapted from the contemporary lute and viol; in French, "accouplement des cordes." The lowest octave was usually restricted to keys carrying one tangent only, and frequently the last notes in the treble were so treated—the beginning of the "bund-frei" or "fret-free" principle, which gradually extended until an entirely unfretted clavichord came to pass—an invention attributed to Daniel Faber, of Crailsheim in Saxony, about 1720. A change so important increased the size and power of the instrument, although never to make it loud, and gave each pair of unisons its own key and tangent, thus making it amenable to the equal temperament tuning preferred by J. S. Bach, and of which he availed himself for stringed keyboard instruments. In 1722 he produced a collection of Twenty-four Preludes and Fugues in all the major and minor keys, each note of the chromatic scale being elevated to the position of an independent key-note, and he named this collection "Das Wohltemperirte Clavier"—that is to say, the equally tempered or tuned clavichord, spinet, or harpsichord.

* Mr. Cummings' clavichord, twenty-one notes of forty-two strings, forty-five keys:—

1	2	3	4	5	6	7	8	9	10	11	12	13	14	15	16	17
E	F	F$\sharp$	G	G$\sharp$	A	B$\flat$	c	d	e	f$\sharp$	g$\sharp$	b$\natural$	d^1	f^1	g$\sharp^1$	b$\natural^1$
						B$\natural$	c$\sharp$	d$\sharp$	f	g	a	c^1	d$\sharp^1$	f$\sharp^1$	a^1	c^2
											b$\flat$	c$\sharp^1$	e^1	g^1	b$\flat^1$	c$\sharp^2$

18	19	20	21
d^2	f^2	g$\sharp^2$	b$\natural^2$
d$\sharp^2$	f$\sharp^2$	a^2	c^3
e^2	g^2	b$\flat^2$	

Mr. Southgate's clavichord, twenty-five notes of fifty strings, fifty-one keys:—

1	2	3	4	5	6	7	8	9	10	11	12	13	14	15	16	17
C	C$\sharp$	D	D$\sharp$	E	F	F$\sharp$	G	G$\sharp$	A	B$\flat$	c	d	f	g$\sharp$	b$\natural$	d^1
										B$\natural$	c$\sharp$	d$\sharp$	f$\sharp$	a	c^1	d$\sharp^1$
												e	g	b$\flat$	c$\sharp^1$	e^1

18	19	20	21	22	23	24	25
f^1	g$\sharp^1$	b$\natural^1$	d^2	f^2	g$\sharp^2$	b$\natural^2$	c$\sharp^3$
f$\sharp^1$	a^1	c^2	d$\sharp^2$	f$\sharp^2$	a^2	c^3	d^3
g^1	b$\flat^1$	c$\sharp^2$	e^2	g^2	b$\flat^2$		

This instrument is inscribed *Peter Hicks Fecit*, and may be accepted as English. The length is four feet, width fourteen inches, depth four inches, black natural keys, and the sharps covered with thin slips of ivory.

The fret-free or chromatic scaled clavichords, five feet or more in length, and of five octaves or more in compass, were in general use in Germany in the middle of the last century, and were made there until about the year 1812. Then the manufacture ceased. Two, however, were made by one Hofmann, in Stuttgart, for Mr. Joseph Street, an English amateur, about the year 1857; and in 1879 Mr. G. J. Chatterton, of London, incited by my article upon the Clavichord, which had then appeared in Sir George Grove's Dictionary, successfully transformed an old square piano into one—the reverse process to that which obtained in Germany about the middle of the last century, when clavichords were converted into square pianos, which was easily done owing to the depth of the sound-box. A re-introduction of clavichord making is due to Mr. Arnold Dolmetsch, of London, who, in 1894, succeeded in again making this delicate instrument. The first was acquired by Mr. J. A. Fuller Maitland, of London, and the second by Sir George Grove for the Royal College of Music at South Kensington. In fact, the square piano so completely supplanted the clavichord that after 1830 pianists had utterly forgotten its peculiar tone and technique, and the name was misunderstood and supposed to mean an instrument of the spinet or harpsichord kind. Even Fétis seems to have had no near knowledge of it by the erroneous conception he had of the "gebunden" clavichord.* He supposed the variation in pitch of the same string was caused in some incomprehensible way by the different bridges on the belly. The first to bring the clavichord back into notice was the late Carl Engel;† he acquired specimens for his collection and let me have one of them for study, and to show musicians who might be curious to learn its special characteristics. In that way and at that time (1874-9) some of the leading pianists of the day had the opportunity to become acquainted with the favourite instrument of J. S. and Carl P. E. Bach. In lectures and recitals on old keyboard instruments in London, Oxford, and Cambridge, given between 1883-93, I have had the privilege to make the clavichord still more known.‡

* Fétis, "Histoire Générale de la Musique," Vol. V., p. 31, and Rimbault, "The Pianoforte," also described without understanding it, as he figures its simple action with the damping cloth on the wrong side of the tangent.
† Engel, pp. 274, 275, 355-357.
‡ "Proceedings of the Musical Association. Twelfth Session, London, 1885-6. Lecture by A. J. Hipkins on the "Old Clavier or Keyboard Instruments: as to the necessity of a legato style of performance," p. 145.

Although never intended to be heard out of the study or a quiet sitting-room, owing to its very tender, intimate *timbre*, I have not hesitated to bring it before large audiences, who have willingly given the attention required and appreciated the charm inherent in its gentle tone.

No great attention seems up to the present time to have been evoked in France, Belgium, or Germany about the clavichord; but in the United States, Mr. Morris Steinert, of New Haven, Connecticut, has, since 1880, taken it up and done much to bring it under the notice of musicians in America.*

A few words may be added about the double clavichord, called a Cembal d'Amour, invented by Gottfried Silbermann. In this instrument the row of tangents came up to the strings at the half of their full vibrating measure, leaving an equal vibrating section on either side. There were, of course, two sound-boards. This division necessitated independent systems of dampers to be raised to the strings, instead of the simple interwoven tape or cloth.† About this time, however, it was attempted to introduce separate damper, shifting, and other stops in the clavichord, and, a little later, knee pedals or genouillères were quite unnecessarily attached to an instrument that, in its "bund-frei," or unfretted form, was almost ideally complete in its simple construction.

VIRGINAL OR SPINET.

These names have been given in this country to one and the same instrument, without regard to the form it was made in, whether trapeze, oblong, or wing-shaped; but were limited nearly always to a plectrum (Jack) clavier with one string only to each note. The earliest recorded name of it is Clavicymbolum, and it occurs under date of 1404 in the rules of the Minnesingers, already mentioned. This name is Latin for a psaltery, an instrument of the dulcimer

---

* Steinert, Morris, "The Renaissance of Joh. Seb. Bach's method of playing the Clavichord" (The Steinert Collection of keyed and stringed instruments), New York, 1893. Reprinted in the "International Exhibition for Music and the Drama." Vienna, 1892. Edited by A. J. Hipkins, F.S.A., Morris Steinert, and Siegmund Schneider. Vienna, 1894.

† Adlung, "Musica Mechanica Organoedi," II., 123-125, with a footnote and diagram added by J. F. Agricola.

kind to which a keyboard was added. It suggests an ecclesiastical or monastic origin. We have it in other forms, as Clavicembalo (Gravecembalo), Italian; Clavecin, French; Clavisinbanos, Spanish; and Clavisingel, Flemish; we find it in English as Clavisymbal in the time of the Tudors. Under date of A.D. 1492, one Clyffe bequeaths his "Clavisymballes";* but this name was afterwards nearly always restricted to the larger harpsichord. The earliest Italian mention of such an instrument occurs in 1461. Sesto Tantini, an instrument maker of Modena, applied by letter for payment of a "Clavicinbalo" supplied to Duke Borso d'Este.† But, as already said, in the confusion of names which too often attends musical instruments, the spinet or virginal was at one time called Clavicordo, Clavicordio, or Clavicorde in Italy, Spain, and France, where the true clavichord was at that time known as Manicordo, Manicordio, and Manicorde. Fortunately, this confusion did not extend to England, except that harpsichords were sometimes included among virginals. Those who come across old notices of keyboard instruments will do well to bear in mind the varying attributions of these names during the sixteenth and seventeenth centuries, in the Latin countries especially.

Virginal was the English name of the spinet, according to the definition of a plectrum keyboard instrument with no more than one string to a note. It would appear to have been given, not as has sometimes been said because Queen Elizabeth was a skilful performer upon it—inasmuch as the name was current in the reign of her grandfather, Henry VII.—but because it was an instrument considered appropriate for girls, the contemporary lute being the more difficult and manly instrument. According to Scaliger,‡ who was born in 1484, the name spinet came from the introduction of the little quill points or plectra, an invention he places in his boyhood and an improvement upon the instruments previously known as monochordum and harpichordum. How their sounds were produced Scaliger does not tell us; we may, however, accept monochordum as a clavichord, and harpichordum as a keyboard psaltery of a harp-shaped disposition, like the English harpsichord. From the little crow-quill plectrum, bearing some resemblance to a thorn (*spina*,

---

* Dr. Murray's New English Dictionary.
† Valdrighi, "Nomocholiurgrafia" (Modena, 1884), p. 243.
‡ Scaliger, ' Poetices," Lib. I., cap. 48. Lyon, 1561.

Latin), Scaliger derives the, in his day, new name of the instrument, spinetta, which remains in Italy to the present day; the French *épinette*, formerly *espinette*, having a like derivation from *épine* or *espine*.

But another origin for the name spinet has been of late years brought forward by an Italian expert, Signor Ponsicchi.* He attributes it to a Venetian maker, who signed and dated such an instrument " IOANNES SPINETUS, VENETUS FECIT ; A.D. 1503," his authority being D. Adriano Banchieri,† who says : " The spinet (spinetta) received this name from the inventor of the oblong shape. He was one Master Giovanni Spinetti, a Venetian, and I have seen one of those instruments in the hands of Francesco Stivori, organist of the great community of Montagnana." Then follows the inscription as above. A portrait of a spinet maker of the early years of the sixteenth century, by an unknown painter, was shown by Mr. Salting in the Exhibition of Venetian Art at the New Gallery, London, in 1894-5,‡ as a possible portrait of Spinetus. The spinet in this painting has the short octave, G, C, A, B, D, E, F. Both derivations of the name refer to about the same date and may be reconciled if, instead of deriving the name of the instrument from Spinetti, the maker, we suppose he adopted his surname from the kind of instrument he made. A little later on we meet with Marco dalle Spinette or dai Cembali, and other instances of this custom.§ It must, however, be remembered that Banchieri was writing a hundred years after the fact he recorded, and he did not claim the invention of the plectrum for Giovanni Spinetti, but that of placing an already existing instrument in an oblong case. The Bologna Exhibition of 1888|| brought to light a spinet of the usual Italian pentagonal model in which there was inscribed the date 1490, the "0" perhaps a little doubtful. It was lent by Count Manzoni and bore the inscription of Alessandro Pasi, of Modena.

* Cesare Ponsicchi, " Il Pianoforte, sua origine e sviluppo " (Florence, 1876), p. 17.

† Banchieri, D. Adriano, " Conclusioni nel suono dell' organo." Bologna, 1609.

‡ Catalogue of the Exhibition of Venetian Art, p. 17, No. 85.

§ Rimbault, " The Pianoforte," p. 399.

|| Bologna Exhibition Catalogue, 1888. " Parte Storica," *Spinetta*. Autore: Alessandro Pasi, Modenese, 1490. Espositore: Sig. Conte L. Manzoni.

The evidence of this, the oldest spinet with a date yet known, may antedate Scaliger a few years; we should not, however, place too implicit a reliance upon Scaliger's statement, which could not have been intended as documentary. But until an older oblong spinet is forthcoming Banchieri's claim for Giovanni Spinetti, that he adapted a trapeze or pentagonal instrument to an oblong case, is so far unaffected. The oldest Italian oblong spinets prove that the pentagonal-shaped spinet was simply enclosed in an oblong box or case, the spaces left at the corners not being filled up. That the instruments of Scaliger's boyhood, whatever they were in structure or form, were known in the fifteenth century is also proved by the discovery of Mr. Edmond Vander Straeten in the Alcazar of Segovia in Spain,* of a testamentary inventory, dated 1503, of musical instruments that had belonged to Queen Isabella, wherein occurs " Dos Clavicinbanos viejos "—two old clavecins or spinets, even then reckoned old! A few years later, and in different countries, there are frequent references to the spinet. One concerns the Chevalier Bayard, wounded at the siege of Brescia in 1509, and carried to the house of a nobleman whose wife and daughters nursed him and entertained him during his convalescence by singing to him and playing upon the lute and " espinette."† The spinet had by that time risen in the favour of the cultivated to rank with the lute. In the household accounts of Margaret of Austria occurs‡ :—

A ung organiste de la ville d'anvers, la somme de vi livres auquel madicte dame en a fait don en faveur de ce que le XVe jour d'Octobre XVXXII. (1522) il a amené deux jeunes enfans, filz et fille, qu'ils ont jouhé sur une espinette et chanté à son diner.

A l'organiste de Monsieur de Fiennes, sept livres dont Madame lui a fait don en faveur de ce que le second jour de Décembre XVXXVI. (1526) il est venu jouher d'un instrument dit espinette devant elle à son diner.

There is, later, the dedication by Clement Marot (Lyons, 1551), on his version of the Psalms to his countrywomen :—

> Et vos doigts sur les Espinettes
> Pour dire Saintes Chansonettes.

These references to the instrument in England would have been

---

* Vander Straeten, "La Musique aux Pays-Bas," Vol. VII., p. 246.

† "Histoire du Gentil Seigneur de Bayard." Composé par le loyal Serviteur. Edition rapprochée du Français moderne par Lor-dan Larchey. Hachette, Paris, 1882.

‡ Vander Straeten, Vol. I., pp. 274-5.

translated virginal. There is a very early reference to the virginal in one of the Leckington proverbs* :—

> A slac strynge in a Virginall soundithe not aright,
> It doth abide no wrestinge (tuning), it is so loose and light;
> The sound-borde crasede, forsith the instrumente,
> Throw misgovernance, to make notes which was not his intente.

To quote from some lexicographers:† Florio's "New World of Worlds" (1611): Spinetta, a kind of little spina; also a pair of virginalles. Spinettegiare, to play upon virginalles. John Minshen's "Doctor in Linguas," 1617: "Virginalls," "Instrumentum Musicum propriè Virginum . . . so called because virgins and maidens play on them; Latin, Clavicymbalum, Cymbaleum Virginæum." And from Blount, "Glossographia," 1656: "Virginal (virginalis), maidenly, virginlike, hence the name of that musical instrument called virginals, because maids and virgins do most commonly play on them." Queen Elizabeth was an accomplished player on this instrument. Her sister, Queen Mary, is reputed to have equalled, if not surpassed her; she played upon the regals and lute, as well as the virginals. Their father, Henry VIII., played well upon the last named, and had a professional virginalist, John Heywood, attached to the Court, who became one of Edward the Sixth's three virginal players. Queen Mary Stuart was also an accomplished virginal player. The virginal that is associated with Queen Elizabeth is now in South Kensington Museum, and may be described as an Italian pentagonal spinet. It bears in its elaborate decoration that Queen's coat-of-arms. The gilding, from an internal date, seems to have been renewed in 1660, and was possibly a restoration of what had been before, or an addition to an instrument known to have belonged to her. The drawing is from the instrument itself when withdrawn from the outer case.

Until about the year 1550, the keyboard was an external addition to the case. Rosso, a Milanese maker, seems to have been the first‡ to set it back in the body of the instrument, a recessing which was afterwards generally followed.

* Rimbault, "The Pianoforte," p. 49.
† "Dictionary of Music and Musicians," "Virginal," A. J. H., Vol. IV., p. 304.
‡ Carl Engel, "Musical Instruments in the South Kensington Museum" (London, 1874), p. 273.

Italian spinets were made of cypress wood, or a kind of cedar, case as well as belly, and the utmost vibration was sought for by the makers throughout. Although the internal work was rough the quality of tone was free and satisfying. It was upon the external case any greater care in workmanship, as well as an often beautiful decoration, were bestowed. The pentagonal or heptagonal spinets had false cases like the clavicembali or harpsichords, from which they could be removed when required for performance; the oblong, in Italy, were, as pianos are now, inseparable from the outer case, and were externally modelled upon the *cassone* or wedding coffers, which had lids, while paintings or other decoration covered the outside. There was such a virginal, or Spinetta Tavola, dated 1568, in the collection of M. Terme, of Liège,* the oldest example known to me; this fashion in virginals was subsequently followed in this country until superseded by the more powerful Spinetta Traversa, the usual English spinet made after the Commonwealth.

According to Mersenne† there were three sizes of "espinette" ("clavicimbalum," as he renders spinet in the Latin edition of that work). One was $2\frac{1}{2}$ feet wide and was tuned an octave above the "ton de Chapelle," or Church pitch,‡ Mersenne's being more than a whole tone higher than the modern diapason normal, or French pitch; one of $3\frac{1}{2}$ feet, a fifth above; and one of 5 feet, tuned to the said Church pitch. Many octave spinets (in Italian, ottavine) are still existing; according to Prætorius their use was for playing with the larger instruments, to give brilliancy to the effect. In the Netherlands double spinets were sometimes made in which the normal keyboard was a fixture, while the octave instrument could be withdrawn. Mrs. Crosby Brown, of New York, has acquired one in London, to present to the Metropolitan Museum of that city,§ made by the Flemish maker Growvels (Ludovicus Grovvelus),‖ and painted with the story of David's victory over Goliath.

* "Encyclopædia Britannica." ninth edition, 1885, Article "Pianoforte" (A. J. H.). Now at South Kensington and regarded as French.

† Mersenne, "Harmonie Universelle," p. 158.

‡ Ellis, A. J., "History of Musical Pitch," p. 382; and Helmholtz, second English edition, p. 503.

§ Catalogue of the Vienna Exhibition, British Section, 1892, A. J. Hipkins, p. 37.

‖ "Recherches sur les Facteurs de Clavecins et les Luthiers d'Anvers," Léon de Burbure (Brussels, 1865), p. 25. Haus Growvels became a Master of the Guild of St. Luke in 1579.

Another, by Hans Ruckers the elder, also decorated with paintings that was exhibited by Mr. George Donaldson in the Inventions Exhibition, 1885,* has also gone to America, acquired by Mr. Steinert. A third, made by Martin vander Beest, and dated 1580, is at Nuremberg.† Again, octave spinets were fitted into the bent sides of harpsichords; a well-known specimen is in the Plantin Museum, Antwerp. The general adoption of an octave stop in the harpsichord did away with the necessity for these contrivances. All, as I have said under Keyboard, were, similarly to clavichords and organs, tuned on the short octave principle in the bass. The apparent compass of the octave spinet was usually three octaves and a sixth, from E to c^3; of the larger instruments, four octaves E to f^3, or $\underline{B}$ to c^3, but really extended to the lowest C or $\underline{G}$ by the short octave expedient.

With the Restoration in England the name virginal went out, the French designation contracted to spinet (spinnet) being adopted; and the transverse or wing form, with the tuning-pin block immediately over the keys, came into vogue. Haward, Stephen Keene, and Thomas Hitchcock appear, by the number of instruments which have come down to us, to have been the most eminent makers; Thomas Hitchcock was succeeded by John, probably a son or near relation. To Haward belongs the distinction of having supplied a spinet, on a triangle stand, to the very musical Samuel Pepys. Among other entries in his Diary concerning this purchase, occurs:—July 15, 1668. "At noon is brought home the espinette I bought the other day of Haward, costs me £5." Haward's shop was in Aldgate, London. Keene, between the years 1672 and 1716, judging from existing specimens, made very beautiful instruments. Thomas Hitchcock's written dates found within instruments made by him cover the long period between 1664 and 1703. He was the first to number his instruments, in which practice John Hitchcock followed him, continuing his numerical series. The spinet in the illustration is numbered 1676,‡ and was given by Handel to a friend

* "Musical Instruments, Historic, Rare, and Unique," by A. J. Hipkins, plate XX., drawn by W. Gibb.

† Reissmann, Dr. August, "Illustrirte Geschichte der Deutschen Musik.' Leipzig, 1881.

‡ *Athenæum,* "Handel's Harpsichords," A. J. Hipkins, No. 2,917, September 22. 1883, pp. 378-9; and *Musical Times* under the same title, December 14, 1893. pp. 30-33.

named Leamon (perhaps Anglicised from Lehmann), who came with him from Germany and ultimately settled in Norfolk, and from his descendants it came into my possession.

The Hitchcocks made their spinets with the then unprecedented compass of five octaves, from $\dot{\text{G}}$ to g^3. They abolished in their instruments the sound-holes in the bellies with the beautiful " knots " or " roses " cut in them ; and in both harpsichords and spinets they inserted in the sharps or raised keys slips of the colour and material of the naturals. In Mr. Boddington's

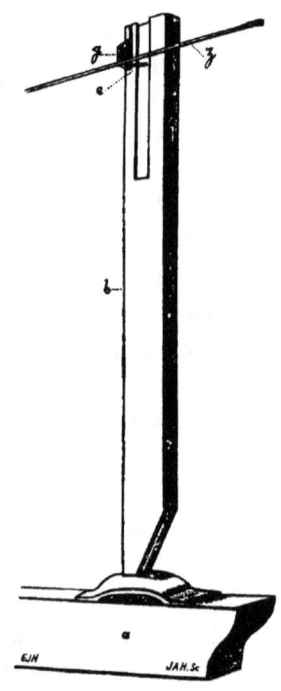

SPINET OR HARPSICHORD JACK.

Collection there is a Haward spinet,[*] dated or numbered 1687, with black naturals and white sharps, the latter with a strip of black in them; even the great London harpsichord maker, Shudi (Tschudi), showed his approval of this fashion by adopting it in the harpsichords he made in 1766 for Frederick the Great's New Palace at Potsdam. There were other favourite spinet makers

---

[*] " Catalogue of Musical Instruments, principally illustrative of the History of the Pianoforte; the property of Henry Boddington." Collected by J. Kendrick Pyne (Manchester, 1888), No. VIII.

during the last century, among whom Slade, Baudin, Mahoon (one of whose harpsichords appears in Hogarth's "Rake's Progress"), and Harris may be named. The latest date I have for a spinet made in London is 1784. It was probably the last made anywhere, until Metzler and Co. constructed one for Mr. Charles Wyndham a few years ago.

Whatever form the spinet or virginal may take, the apparatus for exciting the sound is always the same. On the back end of a balanced key-lever is placed a jack—in the diagram b—a wooden upright, usually of pear-tree, having a centred tongue of holly kept in its place by a spring of bristle behind the tongue. A spike or cutting of crow-quill, e, projects at a right angle from the tongue. The depression of the front end of the key-lever sends the jack up and the little plectrum twangs the string z. As the key regains its level the jack descends, the plectrum passing the string without pressure to again cause sound. The bristle spring is to let the plectrum escape the spring and leave it vibrating, to be damped (silenced) by a small piece of cloth, g, attached to the jack above the quill, which falls upon the string as the key rises to its level. Raven quill has been employed, also buff leather, as is frequently found in old Italian instruments; in the oldest Italian jacks metal springs were used instead of bristles, and possibly metal plectra, of which I have found an example in the upright spinet in the Donaldson Museum. Jack is a common name for a wooden bar or lever (there is the familiar jack-plane). Shakespeare uses it in the oft-quoted sonnet:—

> Do I envy those jacks that nimble leap
> To kiss the tender inward of thy hand;

but in the sense of the key-lever,* not the plectrum or quill jack.

The name of virginal has had very little currency upon the Continent, but an interesting communication made by the late Professor Spitta (the biographer of Bach) to Dr. Carl Krebs,† which I will quote, gives the German word "Frauenzimmer" (Lady) as an equivalent to virginal. "In a concert piece by Heinrich Schütz (1585-1672), 'Veni, Sancte Spiritus,' with four choirs, the instrument playing the 'continuo' to each is designated. To the first the Positive (small stationary organ), to the second 'in the choir' (with the large organ), to the third 'Frauenzimmer,' which, as a

* A planed-up rail (Jack Plane). † Krebs, p. 114.

keyboard instrument, we may translate virginal." Dr. Krebs regards this work as written 1610-20.

The earliest to write upon modern musical instruments, Sebastian Virdung,* figures an oblong instrument under the name; it only differs from the clavicimbalum, so far as can be seen in a very imperfect woodcut, in the compass of the keyboard, a difference of no importance, excepting that the clavicymbalum bass octave is "*mi, re, ut,*" or short octave.† Prætorius, in "Syntagma Musicum" (1618), gives the name "spinetta" to the quadrangular spinet in England and the Netherlands, and figures it accordingly in "Sciagraphia," allotting the name virginal to an hexagonal spinet. Opposed to this definition it has been customary of late years to regard the quadrangular or oblong spinet as the special virginal; I have not found elsewhere the use of the name in the Netherlands, where it is, and has been, either known as "Vierkante clavisingel," or, in French, "Clavecin rectangulaire."

CLAVICYTHERIUM OR UPRIGHT SPINET.

Italian—Spinetta Verticale.

The name Clavicytherium has been applied to a spinet turned up on the broad end, and placed upon a stand of the height required for performance on the keyboard. The strings are single and are set in vibration by a little plectra of quill or leather, as in the horizontal spinets, the jack being set forward by means of an intermediate rail and crank which recedes as the key regains its equilibrium. Virdung (1511)‡ describes the clavicytherium as a new invention with gut strings, but as he had only seen one, and his acquaintance with keyboard instruments was incomplete, too much stress should not be laid upon his description of the upright gut strung instrument he calls by this name; while the figure he gives is of no great value when we have so perfect a specimen as that existing in the wire-strung clavicytherium in the Donaldson Museum at the Royal College of Music. There is a woodcut of a clavicytherium in

* Virdung, B.
† Girolamo Diruta's "Transilvano, ein Beitrag zur Geschichte des Orgel und Klavierspiels im 16 Jahrhundert," von Carl Krebs (Leipzig, 1892), pp. 15-56.
‡ Virdung, B.

Prætorius. The rare instrument in the Donaldson Museum came, in 1885, from the Correr Collection at Venice; it was obtained through the intervention of Mr. Edward Heron Allen, who was one of the foreign commissioners for the Loan Collection attached to the Inventions and Music Exhibition of 1885,* for exhibition in the Royal Albert Hall, Kensington Gore. In this example we have one of the oldest existing specimens of the spinet kind.

Although without a date we are justified by the form and decoration in placing it early in the sixteenth century, if not at the end of the fifteenth. The decorative features are early Renaissance with Gothic features, while the remains of the Calvary inside recalls the art of Mantegna. It may be of North Italian origin, but some writing with which the joints of the back are covered inside is in German, and has reference to an agreement or lease appertaining to Ulm, which may point to Augsburg for the origin of this once beautiful clavier. The case appears to be pinewood; the natural keys are boxwood, which was used for keyboards before ivory, the sharps are of a darker wood and inlaid. The compass represents three octaves and a third, from E to g^2, but is to be taken according to the short octave as having been from C to g^2. The jacks have the early steel springs, and some traces of original brass plectra were found in it in 1885; the use of this metal may have preceded that of quill or leather. The instrument stands upon a stool of later date. It has been admirably drawn by Mr. William Gibb† without attempt at restoration. It is uncertain whether we may apply the name Clavicytherium to the upright harpsichord (clavicembalo), which was occasionally made. Such an instrument, of later date than the rare specimen in the Donaldson Museum, has lately been acquired in Italy by Mrs. J. Crosby Brown, of New York, for presentation to the Metropolitan Museum of that city. The outer case, as frequently happens, has been an addition to the instrument which I attribute to the later years of the sixteenth or earlier of the seventeenth century. The keyboard has the customary forty-five keys, E—c^3 (really C—c^3), of the Italian quilled instruments, and there is an ornamental rose in the sound-board. As

---

* Guide to the Loan Collection, International Inventions Exhibition (A. J. Hipkins, London, 1885), p. 85; and Donaldson Museum Catalogue, 1896.

† "Musical Instruments, Historic, Rare and Unique" (Clavicytherium), by A. J. Hipkins. A. & C. Black. Edinburgh and London, 1888.

the beautiful outer case has not been elsewhere described, I will give some details of its decoration, the paintings being of the Eclectic School, about the middle of the seventeenth century. The outer case does not follow the lines of the clavicembalo, but rises rectangular like a bookcase. The vacant space inside left from the bent side of the instrument is filled up with a painting of King David, crowned and playing upon a harp. The folding doors inside are each in two compartments, representing a singer and players, attended by amorini, of the transverse flute, viol, viola da gamba, and violone. All the principal figures are women. On the board above the keys are amorini singing. On the inside of the hinged wooden flap to cover the keyboard, other amorini dancing to the music of a lutenist. In the four compartments outside the folding doors are players on the lute, trombone, and harp. Outside the sloping flap are amorini supporting, it appears to me, the armorial shield of the owner. The instrument stands upon a podium or table with fluted legs, and the impression conveyed to the beholder by this unique instrument is one of satisfaction due to the simple and refined scheme of proportion, nearly always absent in modern keyboard instruments.

HARPSICHORD.

The harpsichord is a double, triple—in some instances, quadruple—spinet, the sounds being excited by a jack and quill plectrum the same as in the spinet or virginal. In other words, instead of one string to a note, as in the spinet or virginal, the harpsichord has two, three, and sometimes, although rarely, four. Excepting the common features of the case, sound-board, wire strings, and key board, the harpsichord differs entirely in sound excitement and effect from the clavichord. It has an individuality of tone which the pianoforte has not, and a certain power, somewhat grandiose, and brilliancy of effect which the clavichord has not; but in expressive character depending upon the finger, it remains far behind either—indeed, some would deny the harpsichord any expression from the finger. I cannot, however, go with them, as touch must be reckoned with as producing some tone modification, however slight. It is, however, incapable of appreciable accent, a want which affects the *tempi* of rapid passages, and in this respect assimilates the harpsichord to the organ. The importance of the harpsichord during the sixteenth and seventeenth centuries was very great. Where the grand piano would now go, the harpsichord went ; and while not so much a solo instrument, its importance in the orchestra of the time was very great ; the development of the *continuo* or thorough bass, as well as the accompaniment of recitative, being chiefly under the control of the harpsichord player, who assumed the responsibility of conductor.

The complex nature of the harpsichord required a larger and a differently shaped case to that of the spinet, the grand piano being prefigured by it. From this peculiarity of form the Germans called it Flügel, or wing; also Kielflügel, from the plectrum ("Kiel," quill) causing the sound production. The Dutch, Flemish, and French named it from the tail or long continuation, Staartstuk, Clavecin à queue. The Italians, accepting Spinetta for the monochordal clavier, retained Clavicembalo (often corrupted to gravecembalo) for the larger "stromenti di penna," the quilled instruments. The French rejected the last syllables and described by Clavecin what we call harpsichord, while occasionally using the same word with the adjective " carré," or " rectangulaire," for the smaller épinette or spinet. The old name Harpichordum (Arpicordo)* survives in the English harpsichord, the introduction of the sibilant being a mere lingual addition. (It was at one time in England frequently corrupted to harpsicon.)

. We find in the name a recognition of the harp shape, the longer bass strings requiring the harp disposition rather than the trapeze one of the spinet. Galilei says† the harpsichord was so named because it represented an Arpa Giacente or " couched (lying down) harp." The harpsichord appears nearly as early as the spinet ; in order of time there is very little between them. Possibly an extract from the accounts of the Hospital of St. Jean, at Bruges, under date of 1404-5, concerning the pawning of a large " Clavecin " for eight livres for as many weeks, published by Van de Casteele in

* *Musical Times*, 1894, No. 620, Oct. 1, p. 663 ("Radino," by M. L. A.), "Il Primo Libro d'intavolatura di Ballo d'Arpicordo di Gio: Maria Radino, organista in S. Gio, di Verdara in Padova. Nuovamente Composti, e con ogni diligenza Stampati. In Venezia Appresso Giacomo Vincenti. MDXCII."

† Galilei. " Dialogo della Musica Antica e Moderna." Venice, 1583.

a journal called "La Plume," may refer to an early harpsichord.* There is a very fine example in a Roman one at South Kensington Museum, inscribed and dated "Hieronymus Bononiensis Faciebat Romæ, MDXXI." It has one keyboard, and two unison strings to each note; boxwood natural keys, with an apparent compass of nearly four octaves, E to d^3, which by a short octave in the bass becomes C to d^3. Another, nearly as old, is the rare and beautiful specimen in the Donaldson Museum at the Royal College of Music, inscribed and dated "Opus Alexandri Trasuntino, MDXXXI.,"† also with one keyboard and two unison strings. The apparent compass is $\underline{B}-c^3$, just exceeding four octaves; but the real compass was $\underline{G}-c^3$, four octaves and a fourth. Here are ivory natural keys. These instruments of 1521 and 1531 are removable from their elaborate cases, to which we may owe their preservation; although many harpsichords were broken up for the sake of their often beautiful paintings and other decorations. There was no change of power in these Italian instruments attainable by stops, or even later in such "Clavicembali," the Italians being conservative in musical instrument making, and indisposed to adopt changes. The pedals to the Trasuntino harpsichord, controlling a sordino for muting, are a very late addition. Signor Kraus's‡ clavicembalo, made by Domenicus Pisaurensis, is dated 1533. About that time there must have been many such harpsichords made in Italy.

To turn to records, there are details of virginals in England that include harpsichords under that general designation for keyboard instruments. In the Privy Purse expenses of Henry VIII.§ there is an entry: "1530 (April) item the vj daye paied to William Lewes for ii payer of Virginalls in one coffer with iiii stoppes, brought to Greenwiche iii li . . . and for ii payer of Virginalls in one coffer brought to the more‖ other iii lv. And for a little payer of Virginalls brought to the more xxs . . . vii li;" I should say these instruments were from Antwerp, or it may be Cologne, also an early seat of harpsichord and spinet making. The first of these instruments I assume to have been a double keyboard harpsichord with four stops. An Inventory of Henry VIII.'s musical

* Weckerlin, "Musiciana" (Paris, 1877), p. 89.
† Donaldson Museum Catalogue, 1896.
‡ Catalogue, Musée Kraus, p. 15.
§ Edited by Sir N. H. Nicholas. London, 1827.
‖ "The more": the marsh between Charing Cross and Whitehall, afterwards Scotland Yard.

instruments, compiled by one of that king's lute players, Philip Van Wilder* includes "a payre of new long Virginalls made harp fashion of Cipres, with keys of ivory. . . ." In an inventory of Warwick Castle, 1584, we find " a faire paire of double Virginalls," and in the Hengrave inventory of 1603, " one great payre of double Virginalls," probably harpsichords. The Italian keyboard instruments were made throughout with case and belly of cypress, or cedar wood; not pencil cedar, but a native kind. The Antwerp makers took to deal and used it in a like manner throughout. The conspicuous fact is, that we thus early meet with stops, possibly imitated from the organ, the different registers of which had been already taken out of the original Mixture. I am now disposed to believe that the " Piano e Forte " of 1598, found in the records of the house of D'Este, by Count Valdrighi of Modena,† was a double keyboard harpsichord, a Flemish invention then introduced into Italy. The reference to the " Piano e Forte " occurs in letters written by a musical instrument maker, named Hippolito Cricca or Paliarino, addressed June 27 and December 31, 1598, to Alfonso II., Duke of Modena. In another instance the same authority quotes from a letter addressed to the Duke of Ferrara by Giacamo Alvise, dated March 3, 1595, wherein he speaks of a newly invented harpsichord with two strings to a note forming three varieties of sound; that is to say, either string, or both combined by the use of slides and stops.

The invention, about the year 1600, of the Continuo or thorough bass brought the large harpsichord into a prominent position in the orchestra of that time. The lutes were extended by additional necks into theorboes and arch lutes or chitarroni, and in combination with the large viols and violoni were employed to strengthen

* Harleian MS. 1419, A fol. 200, contains this list of musical instruments remaining at Westminster after the king's death. It mentions "five pairs of double regalles, thirteen of single regalles (? portatives), numerous paires of virginalles, both single and double (? double harpsichords). Two paires of clavicordes, and after naming various stringed and wind instruments, virginals harp fashion (? clavicytherium or upright spinet)."

† Valdrighi, "Musurgiana" (Modena, 1879), p. 17-27; and in the *Musical Journal*, "Boccherini," under title of "Alfonso II. da Este suanotore di pianoforte," No. 4, April, 1879. I resign the opinion that Paliarino's "Piano e Forte" might have been a hammer clavier. See my Lecture on the "History of the Pianoforte," read before the Society of Arts, March 7, 1883. *Journal of the Society*, No. 1,581, Vol. XXXI., p. 397-408, with diagrams.

the already sonorous harpsichord in the performance of the bass part. The *recitativo secco* was supported by harpsichord *arpeggios* upon the figured or harmonised bass, for which the peculiar quality of the harpsichord tone, related in effect to the cimbalon or dulcimer in a modern Hungarian Gipsy band, was well suited. Another Venetian Trasuntino, Vito, made an Archicembalo with four rows of keys and thirty-one keys in each of the four octaves to obtain a complete mesotonic pure third tuning, the instrument, before which the performer stood, being an invention of Nicoló Vicentino.* Pedals were occasionally added still further conforming to the organ.

The palm for excellence in harpsichord-making is due to the famous Ruckers family of Antwerp†—Hans, his son Hans (Jean), and Andries (André), and his grandsons Andries Ruckers and Jan Couchet. I have catalogued in Sir George Grove's "Dictionary of Music and Musicians" seventy existing specimens of these instruments,‡ including some of great beauty of decoration; one by the elder Hans, now preserved in Windsor Castle, an undecorated one, is of great historic interest, as there is reason to believe it is the "large" Ruckers mentioned in Handel's will, bequeathed by him to the elder Smith, the father of his pupil and amanuensis, who, out of gratitude for the continuance of a pension, bequeathed it to King George III., together with all Handel's MS. scores and the bust, by Roubiliac. There is an André Ruckers harpsichord in South Kensington Museum, a donation of Messrs. Broadwood, which, although claimed for the instrument named in the will, appears from the documentary evidence to have been at one time also owned by the younger Smith, and often played upon by Handel, who may have given it to him.§ Hans Ruckers the elder was admitted to the Guild of St. Luke, at Antwerp, as "Hans Ruyckers, Clavisinbalmakerre," in 1575.‖ The earliest instrument I have met with by him is dated

---

* Nicoló Vicentino, "L'antica musica ridotto alla moderna prattica." Rome, 1555.

† Ruckers, "Dictionary of Music and Musicians" (A. J. H.), Vol. III., p. 193.

‡ *Ibid*, Vol. III., pp. 197, 652; Vol. IV., pp. 305, 777.

§ "A Descriptive Catalogue of the Musical Instruments in the South Kensington Museum," by Carl Engel (London, 1874), pp. 279-282; in the small Hand Book, pp. 57-59. Both contain an engraving of the instrument.

‖ "De Liggeren . . . der Antwerpsche Sint Lucasgilde" (The Rolls of the Guild of St. Luke). Rombouts and Van Lerius, Antwerp, 1872.

1590; and the latest of the family, one by his grandson, the younger André, dated 1659; his more famous grandson, Jan Couchet, died in 1655.* The period was therefore not long in which all this splendid work was done; it nearly coincided with the glorious epoch of painting in the neighbouring provinces of Holland, and the masterworks in that art of Rubens and Vandyck, the culmination of the Antwerp school.

But of these seventy examples of Ruckers' clavecins not one of the larger kind can be said to have escaped from alteration of scale and extension of keyboard compass; and not unfrequently a second alteration has taken place, a transformation to be explained by these instruments having been esteemed as much as Cremona violins are now, and kept in use until nearly the end of the last century—as long, in fact, as the harpsichord remained in favour. It has been claimed for Hans Ruckers the elder† that he added the octave register, used steel wire for the treble notes instead of the usual brass, contrived a second keyboard in imitation of the organ, and increased the number of keys from E—c^3 to C—c^3—that is to say, made the short octave in the bass a long or chromatic one down to the lowest note. It does not, however, appear that any of these changes can be attributed to him. The "two pair of Virginalls in one coffer with four stoppes," supplied to Henry VIII. in 1530, casts grave doubts upon the double keyboard being Ruckers' invention. Quirin van Blankenburg, a Dutch musician born in 1654, upon whom Mr. Edmond Vander Straeten has bestowed a chapter in the first volume of his great work,‡ has left upon record some very interesting particulars of the Ruckers' manufacture, difficult, it is true, to understand without technical knowledge and experience, but invaluable for a clear comprehension of what the Ruckers' clavecins originally were. Mr. Vander Straeten has translated the complete extract into French. If there are any technical inaccuracies in the translation I have

---

* Constantin Huygens, "Correspondance et œuvres musicales de," edited by Jonkbloet and J. P. N. Land ("Musique et Musiciens au XVII. siècle"), Leyden, 1882, pp. clxx., clxxi.

† Hulmandel, "Encyclopédie Méthodique" (Musique I., 286).

‡ Quirin van Blankenburg, "Elementa Musica," 1739; and Vander Straeten, "La Musique aux Pays-Bas avant le XIXe siècle," Vol. I., pp. 65-69 (Brussels, 1867). Also Reynvaan, "Muzijkaal Kunst-Woordenboek," Art. "Cembalo," pp. 111-116 (Amsterdam, 1795). Reynvaan follows Van Blankenburg implicitly.

not found them. When Van Blankenburg wrote (1738) the Ruckers family as clavecin makers had passed away many years. He was, however, near enough to their time to have experience of what their instruments originally were. He tells us that from about 1600 to 1630 there were two sizes of the long harpsichord, or clavecin with a tail. Of these the longer was provided with two keyboards, the shorter with one; and there was also the oblong or rectangular clavecin—that is to say, the spinet. My examples, tabulated in the "Dictionary of Music and Musicians," show a length of about 7 feet 4 inches for the longer harpsichord; and for the shorter about 6 feet. Van Blankenburg goes on to describe the longer as having in the upper keyboard three octaves and a semitone, $B-c^3$. The lower keyboard had four octaves and a semitone, $E-f^3$, which the short octave extended to four octaves and a fourth, $C-f^3$. But by the artifice of shifting the lower keyboard down the chromatic scale of stringing the interval of a fourth, the compass of this keyboard became in pitch $G-c^3$; the overflowing keys above c^3, the normal highest note, at the treble end of the keyboard, being thus accommodated. The bass notes wanting to complete the upper keyboard compass were omitted, their place being occupied by a wooden block. The same strings, a note and its octave, the latter attached to the sound-board, served for both keyboards; but with separate jacks for either as registers, which were brought into use, or taken off, by slides which projected beyond the right hand side of the case, with cords attached, after the fashion of the stops of the old Positive organs. If a note of one keyboard was struck, the corresponding note of the other, struck simultaneously, was dumb. Van Blankenburg objects to the short octave in the bass of the upper keyboard on account of the notes crossing each other; it is a proof, he says, of the little heed that was then paid to the filling up of the basses.*
The shorter keyboard harpsichord, like the spinet or oblong instrument, had forty-five keys, apparently three octaves and a sixth, $E-c^3$; but by the short octave, four octaves, $C-c^3$. In a double keyboard harpsichord there were, as I have said, four registers and stops, two for each keyboard, although there were only two strings for each note, the same as I should say there were

* ("Vervulling," "Remplissage.") Vander Straeten, "La Musique aux Pays-Bas," Vol. I., p. 66. See footnote, p. 88.

in Henry VIII.'s double virginal already mentioned, before Hans Ruckers was born.

The shift of a fourth in pitch upon the lower keyboard was to facilitate the frequent transpositions by that interval in the music of that period, marked by a B flat at the signature, so that ordinary players might not stumble through change of fingering. I do not think the reading at that time was so much an impediment.*

About 1650, according to Van Blankenburg, there came to pass the earlier changes. First, by shifting the lower keyboard back, whereby the overflowing keys above c^3 became useless and had to be removed. The pitch was then transposed, as Van Blankenburg says, "fa en ut"—that is to say, a fourth higher, making both keyboards the same pitch; the F key no longer sounding C, but F, while five keys were added to continue the keyboard down to $\underline{B}$. After this re-shifting of the keys the vacant space in the bass of the upper keyboard was dealt with, the wooden block was removed, and new keys were put in to make the compass of both keyboards equal—viz., $\underline{B}$—c^3, or by the short octave, $\underline{G}$—c^3: fifty keys, four octaves and a fourth. A little later a third string was added in unison with the original "cymbal" string, and the octave or "spinet" string, as it was called, was combined with the unisons on the lower keyboard, making this the "forte" keyboard when the three registers were employed; while the upper, the "piano" keyboard, had only one. By this arrangement the fourth and nearest register and its drawstop became, for a while, useless. This transformation of the harpsichord appears to have been really due to Jan Couchet, as will be seen from a letter of which I give a translation written by G. F. Duarte, an influential amateur in Antwerp, to his friend Constantin Huygens.† It reads as follows; the italics are mine:

"SIR,—I have received your favour of February 27. In reply I will offer the following remarks touching the conversation you relate about the large Clavecins [Harpsichords] with one full keyboard as

---

* As early as 1511 Arnold Schlick used an organ that could be transposed a tone in both manual and pedal. *Vide* his "Spiegel der Orgelmacher und Organisten," p. 19 of reprint, Berlin, 1869.

† "Music et Musiciens de XVII. siècle." "Correspondance de Constantin Huygens" (Jonkbloet et Land, Leyden, 1882), pp. clxxi., cxc.-cci.; also the *Hobby Horse* for October, 1888, p. 138; "On some Obsolete Musical Instruments," by A. J. Hipkins.

far as the octave below G, sol, re, ut [should be G, ut, first line of the bass clef]. You will be pleased to observe that I have found the nephew of the late Joannis Rukarts [Jean Ruckers], by name Couchet, who worked with his uncle sixteen years, to be of a much more studious mind, with which my instruction has had much to do, in researches which his already mentioned uncle never cared to meddle with. For we need the rapid manipulation of the keys of the large instruments, to make them sufficiently docile to promptly obey, whereby subtleties and delicacies are revealed, so also concerning the measures of length of the quills, keys, and tangents, as well as the sweetness of the harmony [tone-quality], the thickness and length of the strings, all which things it would take too long to explain to you. The extreme length of the large Clavecins is eight feet, a little less or more. The pitch is Corista [Chorton, Church pitch, about a quarter-tone below French], with three registers, meaning three different strings—to wit, two in unison and one an octave; all three can also be played together as each separately, with and without the octave *like the ordinary clavecins that you mention*, but have a better harmony *through the string at rest which is not played, also vibrating by itself,** making always a sweet tranquil harmony through the leading sound to which it is like, which cannot happen when all three are played together. The second unison string has a rather sharper quality than the other one, which also causes an agreeable sweetness by reason of this being rather more than a straw's breadth longer than the other. The goodness of instruments also depends upon strings being slacker, thinner, and longer instead of thick; so that one can with these three strings make five or six diverse changes of playing, and may be very near as soft in touch as a small clavecin, wherein the greatest art consists, which few masters know. Thus much I have to say concerning the large instruments, of which, up to the present time, four only have been made. The last, the best, have been sold for about 300 and afterwards 20 or 30 gulden less, so that one should have them made expressly. Now in what concerns the short tailed instruments *with a unison, or with an octave*, each having its value, they are generally a note higher in pitch [Kammerton, Chamber pitch, about a note higher than French], and of my former invention some years ago, serving in small rooms for playing Courants,

---

* When the quill plectrum is shifted away from the string, the damper is also withdrawn.

Allemands, and Sarabandes. If you please in this or in other things to command me I will show that I am always your humble servant,
"Antwerp, March 5, 1648."* "G. F. DUARTE.

Passing by Duarte's claims for invention or suggestion, we may attribute to Jan Couchet the addition of the unison string and limitation of the octave string—the little octave, as Van Blankenburg calls it—to the lower keyboard. Jean Ruckers, however, made an eight-foot harpsichord in 1632, and one of seven feet eleven inches that is undated, and André Ruckers one of the abnormal length of eight feet ten and a half inches; but the compass of this instrument extended in the bass to the lowest C̱ of the pianoforte.†

The higher tension of the Ruckers scale, when thus altered, combined with the sharp chamber pitch ‡ of that time, rendered it very difficult, even with the thin wire then used, to keep on the highest treble note, c^3; the vibrating lengths of the unison strings being respectively 6½ and 7 inches. He says the belly bridge had been put back as far as possible; no doubt to gain room for the octave string, which was, as already said, hitched on to the sound-board itself, the latter being strengthened for it by a rail of oak or other hard wood underneath. Van Blankenburg mentions an expedient to relieve the high tension which I myself found employed in the double spinet or virginal by Hans Ruckers the elder, now in Mr. Steinert's collection in America, the scale of which a few years ago, before the instrument was restored, was for both keyboards "si—si," Ḇ—b^2, the keyboards having been shifted a semitone downwards. But as the lowest note of the harpsichords, Ḇ, then became Ḇ flat, an inconvenient key to end upon in the bass, an A̱ was added, thus extending the full number to fifty-one keys, but doing away with the short octave.

* I am indebted to Mr. Victor Mahillon, of Brussels, and to Dr. J. P. N. Land, of Leyden, for valuable assistance in the translation of this interesting old Flemish letter.

† "Dictionary of Music and Musicians," Vol. III., p. 198, Art. "Ruckers" (A. J. H.), the instruments catalogued 19, 24, and 34.

‡ Dr. A. J. Ellis, "History of Musical Pitch," p. 332. I am sorry I cannot accept Dr. Ellis's hypothesis concerning the Kammerton, or chamber pitch of Prætorius. I believe it was no more than a whole tone above the Diapason Normal, or, at most, the pitch of the Halberstadt Organ, about an equal minor third above. I agree, however, with Dr. Ellis's determination of Prætorius's Chorton or Church pitch, as having been approximately Handel's pitch, nearly a quarter of a tone below the Diapason Normal. The high pitch went when the modern orchestra was established, and the viols gave way before the violins.

Van Blankenburg goes on to say that certain dealers deceived the public by altering the shorter keyboard harpsichords into double keyboard instruments, and putting them forth as genuine, whereby the reputation of the makers suffered. It has been already remarked that, in making the lower keyboard the *forte* and the upper the *piano*, the nearest stop (an octave one) had become useless. It appears, in 1708, he owned a harpsichord, made in 1623 by Jean Ruckers (Hans the younger), which had four stops, of which he gives the names, *spinetta, unisonus, cymbalum,* and *octava*,* which, according to the organ, he says, would be named *trompette, bourdon, prestant, octave*. There is a little confusion here, as he mentions an organ stop, the bourdon, usually an octave lower than the harpsichord, although occasionally of eight-foot pitch. His mistake is not, however, of importance. According to Adlung,† Prestant and Principal are one and the same, and may apply to a register of any measure, so long as it is of prime importance and excellence. But we must allow Van Blankenburg's claim to have been the inventor of the Lute stop and perhaps of the Buff. Taking the stops as he names them in their order, the spinetta, the farthest away, was the octave on the lower keyboard; unisonus and cymbalum were the second and third, and when the unisons were brought together, cymbalum, by a prolongation of the wooden jack, remained available for either keyboard. But the fourth, the octava stop, the nearest (*de devant*) had become, as already said, of no use to the player.‡ This was the stop he adapted for the lute by shifting its row of jacks forward until they plucked the cymbalum strings in the lower and medium divisions of the scale about two inches only from the bridge, and much nearer in the treble: and placing it upon the upper keyboard. He gives no name to this new effect, so charming in its delicate, reedy tone quality; but the stop has always borne the name of Lute in England, my authorities being Carl Engel, to whom it came through a Kirkman tradition,§ and a harpsichord I have seen, by Culliford, a well-known maker

* Van der Straeten, Vol. I., p. 69.
† "Musica Mechanica Organoedi," I., p. 123.
‡ It is possible that the complete installation of sympathetic strings in the fine harpsichord by Ring, dated 1700, shown by Herr Klinkerfuss, of Stuttgart, in the Loan Collection of the Inventions Exhibition, 1885, was only a disused register.
§ Carl Engel, "A Descriptive Catalogue," 1874, p. 353.

near the end of the last century, who had this stop so labelled.*
Van Blankenburg further says there can still be added "a lute and
a harp stop," by which I conclude he means the buff or muting
stop obtained by shifting a small pad of buff leather against one of
the unison strings; frequently called "lute" on the Continent,†
but bearing no resemblance in the effect to the peculiarly attractive
tone of that lovely instrument.

Perhaps the nearest to an unrestored Ruckers, although with
renewed keyboards and added "unisonus," is the beautiful harpsichord that belonged to the late Mr. Leyland, of Speke Hall and
South Kensington—a Jean Ruckers, dated 1642. Here the stops
are in the original position at the side of the case, four in number,
and not brought over the keyboard, another contrivance of Van
Blankenburg who introduced the brass knobs since customary.
Two stops act upon the octave string, the farthest and the nearest,
thus answering to the spinetta and octava. The difference in tone
quality from the difference of "striking place" is even here noteworthy, the spinetta being richer and the octava keener.‡

Since writing about Van Blankenburg I have had the good
fortune to find a Jean Ruckers harpsichord, date 1638, the keyboards of which have remained unaltered. The highest note is
c^3 in the upper and f^3 in the lower, the latter being exactly under
the former, the jacks of both touching the same strings, so that
the lower keyboard is a fourth below the upper in pitch. There
is a wooden block at the bass end of the upper one precisely as
described by Van Blankenburg to fill up space that keys might
occupy. The only difference is that his upper keyboard goes down
to B natural and this to E, an unimportant variation. We learn
from Arnold Schlick § that organs were tuned a fourth apart to
effect the same purpose in accompanying the Plain Song, a
transposition to enable the Plagal modes to lie for the voice as
conveniently as the Authentic, and from this the high and low
church pitches arose, at first, as said, a fourth apart, although
later only a minor third or a whole tone, the tendency being to
a compromise. As applied to the harpsichord in the first half of

* "Dictionary of Music and Musicians" (A. J. H.), Vol. III., p. 718.
† Adlung, "Musical Mechanica Organoedi," II., p. 107.
‡ This fine instrument became, in 1896-7, the property of the Countess of Dudley.
§ Spiegel der Orgelmacher und Organisten," Arnold Schlick (Mainz, 1511); and
"History of Musical Pitch," A. J. Ellis (London, 1880). p. 306.

the seventeenth century, this was a survival only, soon to be done away with by Couchet and his contemporaries. Van Blankenburg's objection to the short octave mentioned on page 82, which puzzled Mr. Vander Straeten, is explained by a contrivance in this instrument.* Wooden prolongations upon the lowest E, F sharp, and G sharp keys of the upper manual, diverge at an angle to the left so as to hold and raise the jacks of the yet lower C, D, and E, thus obtaining a short octave without upsetting the chromatic order above the short octave of the lower keyboard. A restorer (one has attached a sourdine to the instrument), before the beautiful decoration which adorns it was added, has removed two of the rows of jacks and plugged up the openings where their rails or slides would project at the right hand side of the case, thus converting

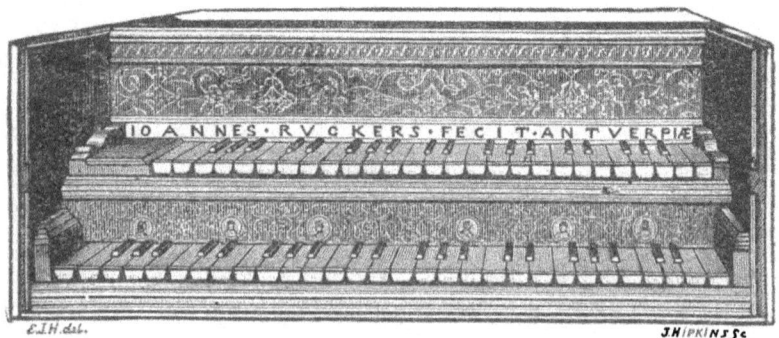

KEYBOARDS OF HARPSICHORD BY JEAN RUCKERS, A.D. 1638.

the instrument into a double spinet, with the lower keyboard an eleventh higher in pitch than the upper; a senseless proceeding but not irremediable. This interesting and unique harpsichord belongs to the Right Honourable Sir Bernhard Samuelson. It had been for many years in the possession of Mr. Spence, of Florence. It is possible it went to Italy when first made, which would account for its having remained with the original keyboards. My meeting with it is due to the courtesy of Mr. Kemp, of Messrs. Chappell and Co., who had it to repair.

* Mr. Vander Straeten admitted that he could not translate satisfactorily the passage referring to this contrivance, and quoted, p. 66, the original Dutch text, which I render: "and this with great trouble because the keys . . . must reach crosswise over each other." This harpsichord removes all doubt as to the meaning.

While these radical changes took place in the construction of the harpsichord, and in the ideas controlling its keyboard arrangement and compass, it is remarkable that no change of any importance happened in the sound exciter, the jack with its little plectrum and cloth damper. In a communication from Mr. Charles Meerens, of Brussels, published this year in *La Federation Artistique*, and reprinted in *L'Echo Musical* of that city, Mr. Meerens says : " The replacement of the jack by the hammer offers a curious spectacle of the fecundity of human intelligence. As much as the jack remained stationary during three centuries, so much has the hammer inspired different systems ever since its first appearance in 1709. The number of diverse mechanical actions with their modifications and subsequent improvements cannot be reckoned. On the one hand, we observe among the makers an indolence without parallel so far as the plectrum is concerned ; on the other, we see for the hammer a feverish imagination displayed which never sleeps or ceases to work, and never dries up. . . . Certainly the spirit of imitation is inborn in man, which may explain this faithful constancy to the harpsichord mechanism." That is to say, as first invented. It served its purpose, and perhaps could not have been improved upon.

The next alteration, an eighteenth century one, was to entirely abolish the short octave and make the keyboards " en ravalement " (a lowering, from the French " ravaler ") by an extension of compass that continued the bass in chromatic order to $\underline{G}$ or $\underline{F}$, and thereby, as Van Blankenburg deplores, cramping the scale to the detriment of the tone. The keyboard blocks were reduced or removed, and treble notes were also added.

The originally limited compass of the Ruckers' harpsichords is supported by Sainsbury.* There was a correspondence in 1637-38 between the painter Balthazar Gerbier, at that time at Brussels, and Sir F. Windebank relative to the purchase of a good virginal—that is to say, a harpsichord, from Antwerp for King Charles the First. Gerbier bought one by Jean Ruckerts (*sic*) with two keyboards and four stops, and paintings inside the cover, one by Rubens, for £30, and when sent over it was found to be wanting six or seven keys, and was therefore insufficient for the music intended to be played upon it. Harpsichord or virginal music had at that time assumed

* W. N. Sainsbury, "Original unpublished papers illustrative of the Life of Sir Peter Paul Rubens" (London, 1859), p 209.

a greater development in England than on the Continent. Jean Ruckers was asked to exchange this instrument for one of larger compass, but declined with a curt message that he would not alter the instrument and had not another to supply in lieu of it.

As with Stradivari and the violin, it might not have been so much invention, as a perfect intuition of the means for producing beautiful tone, that raised the Ruckers' family so far above their fellows. The fact remains that hardly two of the Ruckers' instruments that have come down to us are of exactly the same dimensions. Their work must have been always artistic and experimental, not on fixed mechanical lines. It was not uncommon to adorn them with painting and other expensive decoration, even when a hundred years old. From a well-repaired specimen here and there, notwithstanding the alterations spoken of as detrimental to the maker's scale, we may concur in the extraordinary merits of these once much loved instruments.

The greatest harpsichord makers of the eighteenth century were, in London, Burkat Shudi (Burkhardt Tschudi) and Jacob Kirckman (Kirchmann). The former began business, in 1742, in the house occupied for 162 years as the business premises of his descendants, the Broadwoods, 33, Great Pulteney Street,* Golden Square, London. Kirckman has been represented by his family in a London pianoforte manufactory of repute. In Paris, Taskin had a great name, but later in the century. With these makers the cases were no longer of resonant cypress, cedar, or pine; the prevailing style of domestic furniture had led to more rigid cases of walnut and Spanish mahogany. The tone was of greater power and majesty than had previously been attained, and step by step with the orchestra and organ registration, a greater variety of tone by freer use of the stops was sought for. Lastly, perhaps incited by the pianoforte, *crescendo* and *diminuendo* became desiderata, and a swell was introduced for the harpsichord, as seen in Kirckman's harpsichords, by gradually raising the cover with a pedal (an invention of Roger Plenius), and improved upon by Shudi's "Venetian swell,"† the frame of louvres

* *The Daily Advertiser*, Tuesday, October 5, 1742: "This is to give notice that Burkat Shudi, Harpsichord maker to H.R.H. The Prince of Wales, is removed from Meard's Street, in Dean Street, Soho, to Great Pulteney Street, Golden Square."

† Patent No. 947, 1769. A *Salzburger Zeitung*, dated 6 August, 1765, alludes to Shudi's Venetian swell, together with his use of the machine stop, which, from a London report concerning the child Mozart's last concert there, it also attributes to him. See Pohl's "Mozart in London" (Vienna, 1867), pp. 126-7. The patent for the Venetian swell was therefore taken out some years after the invention.

or shutters that was soon afterwards transferred, with so much advantage, to the organ.

But even with the large English harpsichords of Shudi and Kirckman, the wire used was very thin. In a Shudi one, dated 1770, the wire is marked on the bridge with the gauge numbers from four in the treble to fifteen in the bass, down to C. In a contemporary Kirkman it is from four down to thirteen, the lowest note being F. The octave registers begin at four, but are carried down with a somewhat less diameter. The lowest fourteen to seventeen notes are brass, the rest steel.

Some large German harpsichords had not only the two unison registers and an octave one equivalent to eight and four feet stops, but also a Bourdon, answering to sixteen feet pitch. John Sebastian Bach had one of this calibre; it formed one of the interesting objects in Herr Paul de Wit's collection in Leipzig and has been transferred to the Museum attached to the Hochschule für Musik in Berlin.* There is also such an instrument at Brussels.† Bach's use of the two keyboards is shown in his celebrated Goldberg Variations; but in those variations requiring both keyboards eight foot stops only can be used.‡ I have found with a Shudi or Kirckman harpsichord a well-balanced registration, enhanced by a not too prominent contrast of quality, to be with two unisons (eight-foot) on the lower keyboard, against a single eight-foot and lute on the upper. The lute stop, as already said, has the striking place for its plectra very near the wrestplank bridge, causing a "luthée," or we may say, mandoline quality of tone. The other rows, the eight-foot unisons and four-foot octave are contiguous and lower down the string; in all the spinet jack is used, with quill or leather. Shudi and Kirckman followed the later Ruckers or Jean Couchet's example in the arrangement of keyboards and stops, which came to pass through Tabel, to whom Shudi and afterwards Kirckman were foremen, and who, being a Fleming, brought Antwerp

* "Zeitschrift für Instrumentenbau," 10 Jahrg, No. 36 (Leipzig, 1890), pp. 429-32. "Der Flügel Joh. Seb. Bach's." Königliche Hochschule für Musik zu Berlin. "Führer durch die Sammlung alter Musik-Instrumente," von Dr. Oskar Fleischer (Berlin, 1892), p. 111.

† Victor Mahillon, "Catalogue Descriptif et Analytique du Musée Instrumental du Conservatoire Royal de Bruxelles," Tome II., 1re livraison, p. 39.

‡ *Musical Times*, No. 574, December, 1890, pp. 719-22. Mr. Hipkins's Lecture on "The Old Claviers," given at the Oxford University Musical Club.

traditions with him. A pedal of the nature of a composition pedal in the organ, but not really one, inasmuch as it reduced each keyboard to a single register, was introduced about the year 1750 in England, and used in combination with a stop to the left hand of the player. It is this I have referred to in the footnote concerning Mozart and Shudi, page 90. From the harpsichord made by Culliford I am enabled to distinguish it as the "Machine" stop. When the machine or pedal stop is put back and the foot presses down the left pedal, the octave is withdrawn from the lower keyboard and the cymbal (Engel's first unison) from both keyboards, while the lute is put on to the upper. The harpsichord is thus reduced to the lute upon the upper, and the unison (Engel's second unison) upon the lower. Releasing the pedal withdraws the lute, and restores the registers of cymbal on the upper keyboard, with the full power, cymbal, unison, and octave on the lower. When the machine is set forward this combination is fixed and the pedal will not act. The ironwork for this stop is outside the case. A pedal to the right is for the swell. All the simple effects in an Antwerp or English harpsichord are possible with a single keyboard; but the two keyboards permit contrast. All the best English harpsichords were furnished with both lute and buff stops. Shudi placed his left hand stops thus: *lute, octave, buff;* Kirkman, *buff, lute, octave.* The right hand stops controlled the unisons. With Shudi the buff stop modified the second unison string: Kirkman appears to have preferred the cymbal or first unison. The former was better because it allowed the lute on the upper keyboard to be contrasted with the buff on the lower. German and French harpsichords are to be met with in which there is a harp stop with its own row of jacks furnished with very broad leather plectra, besides the usual buff stop. But this is a mere shading of the *pizzicato.*

A harpsichord was made by Clementi—the great pianist and predecessor of the firm of Collard—as late as 1802, which was the last year in which Beethoven's Sonatas were published "for the Harpsichord or Pianoforte."

Since 1888 harpsichords have been made in Paris by the pianoforte makers, Pleyel, Wolff & Cie., and S. & P. Erard. Messrs. Pleyel have introduced original features, one being a substitution of pedals for hand-stops, the gradual depression of which produces a *crescendo*. Messrs. Erard have been content to reproduce a "Clavecin" by Taskin, said to have been made for Marie Antoinette. These instruments, in common with other French and German harpsichords I have met with, differ from the Antwerp (and English) model in having independent strings for the two keyboards. The Sieur de la Barre* (Espinette et Organiste du Roy et de la Reyne) wrote to Constantin Huygens, on the 15th October, 1648, in reply to an inquiry respecting the price of harpsichords in Paris: "For the truth is this gentleman, who is still young, early discovered the invention of making 'Clavesins à deux claviers,' not in the fashion of Flanders, where only the same strings are played, but different, inasmuch as they sound different strings on each keyboard, and properly speaking two 'clavesins' are joined in one and consequently the work is doubled." In Pleyel's harpsichord or clavecin, which was kindly lent for my lectures at Cambridge and London,† 1892-3, there are two registers, one of eight-foot and one of four-foot (octave) pitch on the lower keyboard, and a separate eight-foot one in the upper, all with leather plectra; the pedals acting thus: (lower keyboard from the left) first, leaves the eight-foot sounding; second, the four-foot (upper keyboard); third, a muting or *pizzicato*; fourth, coupling the three registers for the *ensemble* or "*grand jeu*"; fifth, adding the lute or near plucking register gradually, making a *crescendo*; sixth, taking off the lute, making a *diminuendo*. The fifth and sixth put down together produce the lute only. The Erard harpsichord has also two keyboards of five octaves' compass and three rows of jacks, two of leather and one of quill. It has two *genouillères*, or knee levers, instead of hand stops, and two pedals, a *forte* and *sourdine*. The upper keyboard acts upon a leather row of jacks of eight-foot pitch, which speak always when this keyboard is touched. The lower keyboard is for the combinations. The right knee *genouillère* pushed to the right couples both keyboards, eight-foot leather and eight-foot quill; pushed to the left, the octave, or four-foot leather and eight-foot quill. The left knee *genouillère* pushed to the right brings on the eight-foot of the upper keyboard, to the left there is

---

* "Huygens," Ed. Jonkbloet and Land, p. 149.
† *Monthly Journal of the Incorporated Society of Musicians*, Vol. V., No. 2 February 1, 1893. Lecture by A. J. Hipkins, p. 32.

the eight-foot quill register alone. With the right knee lever pushed to the left and the *forte* pedal put down, the three rows of jacks make the *ensemble* or "*grand jeu*" on the lower keyboard, the upper one being brought forward without disturbing the action of the jacks.*

CLAVIORGANUM, OR ORGANISED SPINET.
(Espinette Organisée—Rabelais.)

An early combination was made of the spinet or harpsichord with flute stops of the organ. Mr. Edmond Vander Straeten has discovered a very early Spanish record of an instrument with this name—a Chamberlain of Queen Isabella, named Sancho de Paredes, owned, before 1480, " Dos Clabiorganos "—two claviorgans or organised clavecins.† Rabelais comes next in order of time; his book was published before 1552, and he compares the toes of Carême-prenant to an " espinette organisée."

Spinets with such attachments are not now forthcoming; the exception being one seen by Herr Carl Krebs in the Vienna Exhibition of Music and the Drama in 1892.‡ This instrument, according to his description, closed like a draught-box, from which he was inclined to accept it as the lost Echiquier; it would seem that the organ pipes were on one side and the spinet or clavicymbalum on the other.

Of organised harpsichords there is no want of specimens. To name two, there was a very grand compound instrument of this kind shown by Mrs. Luard Selby, of the Mote, Ightham, Tunbridge, Kent, in the South Kensington Exhibition of Musical Instruments in 1872; § it bears the maker's inscription, " Lodowicos Threwes (? Theewes) me fecit," ‖ and is now in South Kensington Museum.

---

* An old German expedient. See Adlung's " Musica Mechanica Organoedi " for the harpsichord, II., 108; for the clavichord, II., 147.

† Vander Straeten, " La Musique aux Pays-Bas," Vol. VII., 1885, p. 248.

‡ Vander Straeten, " La Fédération Artistique," No. 27.

§ " Catalogue of the Special Exhibition," Carl Engel (London, 1872), p. 38.

‖ Mr. Vander Straeten has recognised this maker in Louis Theeuwes or Teeus, one of the ten harpsichord makers admitted, without masterpieces, in 1558, into the famous Guild of St. Luke at Antwerp. Masterpieces were afterwards indispensable. See " Leon de Burbure," p. 21.

Another was shown in the Loan Collection at the Royal Albert Hall, Kensington Gore, in 1885, with the maker's name, Crang, and dated 1745. Shudi, the harpsichord maker, made such compound instruments occasionally in collaboration with the organ builder, Snetzler. At the Handel Festival which took place in Westminster Abbey in 1784, the harpsichord at which Joah Bates sat was connected with the organ erected for the performance, so that either instrument could be used at the discretion of the player.

Merlin, in London about this time, made square pianos with organ attachments. In the present century the piano has been sometimes combined with the free reed harmonium, but not with the organ.

SOSTENENTE KEYBOARD INSTRUMENTS.

As recently as 1893 a sostenente instrument, resembling a harpsichord in form, was shown to the public in Madrid, inscribed "Fray Raymundo Fruchador, inventor, 1625," that was a simple development of the hurdy gurdy principle, produced by a mechanical apparatus that brought the strings into contact with rotating wheels turned by a handle at the end of the case. This instrument had been used in the Cathedral of Toledo during Holy Week. It is well known that the word "inventor" inscribed on old musical instruments often occurs in the sense of maker, or implies only an alteration or improvement. The question arises—was this in 1625 a novel instrument, or a copy or modification of one already existing? The latter is more likely, and as hurdy gurdy keyboard instruments were in use earlier than that date it is just possible that the two "Clabiorganos" that belonged to one of the Chamberlains of Queen Isabella of Spain in 1500, already referred to, were instruments of this kind, and not harpsichords or spinets with organ attachments. Schroeter, a claimant for the invention of the piano, in an autobiographical sketch, speaks of a "Geigenwerk" (Fiddle organ) from Nuremberg which was worked by treadles. This would be the "nurnbergisches Gambenwerk" (Gamba organ) of Hans Haydn, organist to the Church of St. Sebald, who is recorded to have made, about 1600, a catgut strung harpsichord. In the Gambenwerk, the strings were under the soundboard and were acted upon by resined parchment set in motion by rollers governed by a wheel. We also meet with a Lautenwerk (Lute organ), an instrument which is connected with J. S. Bach, inasmuch as he designed one.* As the pianoforte seems to have been without attraction for him, although in his later years really well made, as the Potsdam grand pianos show, it may have been that this was another attempt at a *sostenente* clavier. We only know that it had gut strings instead of wire. If not a wheel instrument, such things would require very strong plectra, which would render the touch difficult.

The clavicytherium described by Virdung in 1511,† in the specimen seen by him and averred by him to be newly invented, was a gut-strung spinet, turned up vertically, with metal hooks or plectra, but not *sostenente*. A facile touch might not have been then a desideratum, although it certainly was when the English Virginal books came to be written and published, towards the end of the sixteenth and in the early years of the seventeenth century.

Roger Plenius,‡ a harpsichord maker in London, patented in 1741 a new instrument intended for a *sostenente* harpsichord. He called it "Lyrichord," and from his specification and a drawing in a magazine published in 1755, we gather that it was a wheel clavier on the principle of the hurdy gurdy; the strings of wire and gut being set vibrating by rotating wheels, the keys, when pressed down, causing the contact. No doubt the stringing was heavier than in the ordinary harpsichord, as in this patent there is the first employment of steel arches between the wrest-plank and belly rail to keep them from pulling together; in the second patent, dated 1745, there occurs what is technically known as "bushing" the keys (lining the mortises of the keys to prevent rattling); and lastly, a "Welch Harp" stop, a variety of the buff or *sourdine* stop in harpsichords, which he worked by a pedal. The tuning of the Lyrichord was effected by balanced weights and springs; the bass strings were silver covered, and there was a swell

---

* See a footnote of Agricola's in Adlung's "Musica Mechanica Organoedi," II., 139.

† Virdung, B.

‡ Plenius, Patents Nos. 581 and 613.

obtained by raising with another pedal part of the cover of the instrument, a contrivance, as I have said, often met with in Kirkman's harpsichords. Plenius was the first to make a pianoforte in England.

The "Celestina"* of Adam Walker, patented in London in 1772, was also a *sostenente* instrument. What we know of it is chiefly gathered from Mason's correspondence with Mary Granville (Mason was an intimate friend of the poet Gray). Under date of January 11, 1775, she describes it as a short harpsichord in form, only two feet long, played with the right hand while the left controlled a kind of violin bow. Mason played upon it with great expression, and the invention has been attributed to him, but probably with no more reason than that of the English square piano. He may have been the patron whose means and liberality made these inventions practicable.

John Isaac Hawkins, the inventor of the modern upright piano, contrived the "Claviol," which was in form like a cabinet piano, and is said to have had a ring-bow mechanism. He introduced it at Philadelphia, U.S.A., in 1802, and brought it to London in 1813.

Isaac Mott† had more success with a "Sostenente pianoforte," which he patented in 1817. He sustained the tone by means of rollers acting upon silk threads, set in movement by a pedal, and he claimed the power to increase or diminish the tone.

A French invention with a pianoforte keyboard is the "Piano Quatuor," a piano violin capable of rapid articulation, brought out by Baudet in Paris in 1865. Here are vertical wire strings; a stiff piece of catgut projects about an inch from a nodal point in each; a roller rotates near them with great rapidity, but only touches the catgut ties as the keys are put down.

The last to be named is the Organo-Piano of Signor Caldera, the patent for which in the United Kingdom is held by Messrs. Metzler and Co., London. The principle is original as a piece of mechanism, the apparently sustained effect being produced by reiterated blows from small hammers placed above the ordinary hammers, suspended from a bar which is kept in motion by a fly-wheel and pedal controlled by the performer. A crescendo is

---

* Adam Walker, Patent No. 1,020.
† Mott, Patent No. 4,098.

obtained by a knee movement which raises the bar and brings the little hammers nearer to the strings. The sustained tone of music wire has a peculiar charm, but after all that may be said in favour of the *sostenente* in keyboard stringed instruments, with sustained sounds they are pianoforte or harpsichord no longer. The character is changed; a new treatment is demanded and different order of composition. The ideal character of evanescent tone associated with these instruments, and especially the pianoforte. is not there.

Part 3.

HISTORICAL.

THE EARLY PIANOFORTE.

Before the Introduction of Iron in its Construction, 1709—1820.

The first compositions published, so far as I know, for the pianoforte are contained in a volume thus entitled:—" Sonate Da Cimbalo di piano e forte detto volgarmente di Martellatti. Dedicato a Sua Altezza Reale. Il serenissimo D. Antonio Infante Di Portogallo E Composito Da D. Lodovico Giustini di Pistoia. Opera Prima Firenze MDCCXXXII." That is, Cimbalo or Cembalo, with Piano and Forte, commonly called Cimbalo, with little hammers; Cimbalo being originally the Psaltery, or, with hammers, the Dulcimer; it was later employed, but usually as Cembalo, for the Harpsichord.

The invention of the Paduan harpsichord maker, Bartolommeo Cristofori, in Florence, in 1709 or thereabouts, had thus already become so well known as to have Sonatas composed for the instrument, and published as early as 1732, the year after Cristofori died.

The uncertainty which hung over, or was supposed to effect the claim of Cristofori for the invention of the pianoforte, has, in the last few years, been dispelled by the late Cavaliere Puliti, and finally by proof I have been able to bring forward that Frederick the Great's Silbermann pianos at Potsdam are copies which still exist of the Cristofori pianos. There is no other claim either English, French, or German that is now to be seriously considered.*

---

* The claim for the German, Schrœter, has been warmly advocated by Dr. Oscar Paul, " Geschichte des Claviers " (Leipzig, 1868), pp. 85-104, and answered in Sir George Grove's " Dictionary of Music and Musicians," London,

As a matter of fact, the " Gravecembalo col piano e forte," as the inventor called it (Clavicembalo or Harpsichord, with soft and loud, which early became Forte-Piano, and Pianoforte), was first produced by Bartolommeo Cristofori, in Florence, in 1708 or 1709. In the year 1711 Scipione Maffei (in the "Giornale dei Letterati d'Italia") wrote a full description of the invention and gave a diagram of the action.* There are two grand pianos by Cristofori, still existing, dated respectively 1720 and 1726. The first belonged to the Signora Ernesta Mocenni Martelli, of Florence, and has been described and figured by the Cavaliere Puliti; it has (1895) been acquired by Mrs. J. Crosby Brown, of New York, for presentation to the Metropolitan Museum of that city. It is of four and a half octaves, C—f^3, and is in a simple, panelled outer case, like the usual Italian harpsichord. It bears upon the board which serves as the hammer beam the following inscription: " Bartholomæus de Christophoris Patavinus, Inventor, faciebat Florentiæ, MDCCXX."; and also: " Restaurato l'anno 1875, Cesare Ponsicchi, Firenze."† The second, belonging to the Commendatore Alessandro Kraus, also of Florence,‡ I had the opportunity to examine and play upon, when it was at the Trocadero, in the Paris Exhibition of 1878; a complete and agreeable instrument with facile touch when I tried it. The compass of it is four octaves, C—c^3. The engraving which precedes this section represents this now historic instrument. It is in an outer case, red, with Chinese figures and landscapes in gold, a decoration it has not been possible to show in the engraving. The inner side of the top or cover is light blue. It is inscribed " Bartholomæus de Christophoris Patavinus, faciebat Florentiæ, MDCCXXVI.," leaving out the word " Inventor."

1881—" Pianoforte " (A. J. H.). For the Frenchman, Marius, see Rimbault's " History of the Pianoforte " (London, 1860), pp. 102-108. No result followed his invention, and it is doubtful whether he made a pianoforte. It is certain Schrœter did not.

* " Nuova Invenzione d'un Gravecembalo col piano e forte: Aggiunte alcune considerazione sopra gli strumenti musicali." Puliti, " Cenni Storici, Atti Dell' Academia del R. Institute di Firenze, 1874," Allegato C, pp. 85-93. Rimbault, " The Pianoforte," p. 95.

† Puliti, pp. 119-126.

‡ A. Kraus figlio, " Catalogue des Instruments de Musique du Musée Kraus " (Florence, 1878), p. 16, and Trocadero, Historical Exhibition. Paris, 1878. No. 18

THE EARLY PIANOFORTE. 101

The actions of both these instruments are alike, except that the first has had new hammers of modern shape put to it; they are improved upon the diagram given by Maffei—especially by the invention and introduction of the check (paramartello). The diagram here given is from a model I had made of this action; it is evident from it, as well as from the earlier sketch of Maffei, that Cristofori had satisfactorily solved the problem of escapement. It also shows that he had provided for repetition, so far as could be without a double escapement.

a is the key; b the hopper (linguetta mobile—moveable tongue, Cristofori called it), c the notch for the hopper beneath an under-hammer or escapement lever, lettered k. This lever, covered with leather upon the end, is to raise the hammer-butt d. The hammer-head is e.

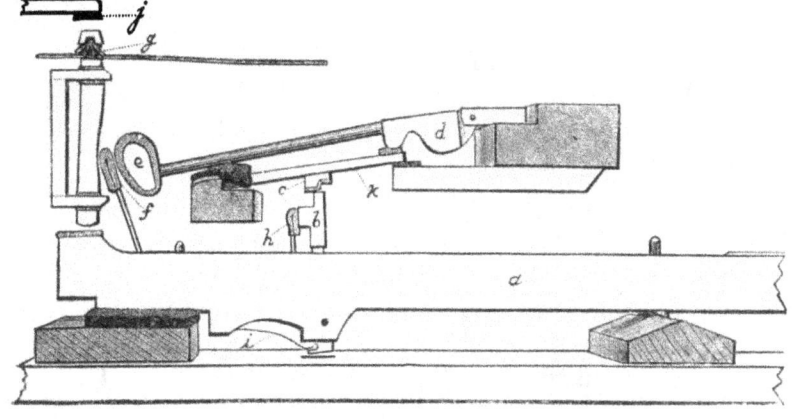

CRISTOFORI'S ACTION.

The spring i, under the key, maintains the position of the hopper in the notch, assisted by the small hopper check, h. The hammer check is f, the damper g. The damper stop is j. It will be observed that the shallowness of Cristofori's case and the thickness of his wrest-plank constrained him to pierce the key with his hopper.

It would seem that Cristofori tried to keep to the shallow measure of an Italian harpsichord, and therefore inverted his wrest-plank, which had necessarily to be much stronger than in the harpsichord, attaching his strings beneath. The pins pierced the wrest-plank so that the tuning was done harp fashion. The spacing of the two unisons of a harpsichord, unlike the pianoforte, brings into proximity two strings a semitone apart. Cristofori did not see his way to the more practical spacing by pairs of unisons; he scaled his pianoforte strings at equal distances, and then dropped a wedge-shaped damper between those that were tuned together. As with the wrest-plank, the thicker strings necessary to withstand the impact of a hammer compelled him to run a strip of oak upon the belly round the inside of the case, whereby to hold the hitch-pins, to which the farther ends of the strings were attached, in order to bear the increased strain. He cut away little openings at the front edge of the belly to replace the customary sound-holes. It is in the retention of sound-holes and also in a more extended keyboard that the grand pianos of Silbermann at Potsdam, of 1746-7, differ from those by Cristofori at Florence. All other peculiarities are retained so far as the inside is concerned. The external case work is, however, changed, being, as in modern pianos, part of the structure. Cristofori had enclosed his in the Italian false case.

The invention, notwithstanding its importance, soon died out in Italy. A pupil of Cristofori, Giovanni Ferrini,* made a pianoforte in 1730 for the Queen of Spain, Elisabetta Farnese, which was left by her to the famous singer, Farinelli, who prized it so highly that he had inscribed upon it in letters of gold "Raffaello d'Urbino," and gave it the first place in his instrumental collection. At that time such collections were formed by eminent personages and much cared for. To Ferrini was left by Cristofori the completion of the instruments he had in hand at the time of his death.

The merit of having taken the invention up and introducing it in Germany is due to Gottfried Silbermann, the great organ builder and clavichord maker of Dresden. Silbermann was the friend of the Dresden Court poet König, who published at Hamburg, in 1725, a translation of Maffei's article in the *Giornale* upon Cristofori's invention.† According to J. S. Bach's pupil, Johann Friedrich Agricola,‡ Silbermann made two pianofortes upon an existing model, the origin of which in his lifetime he would never confess, and submitted them to Bach,§ who, to his great vexation,

* Cesare Ponsicchi, "Il Pianoforte sua origine e sviluppo" (Florence, 1876), p. 37.
† Oscar Paul, "Geschichte des Claviers" (Leipztg. 1868), pp. 105-113.
‡ Adlung, "Musica Mechanica Organoedi" (Berlin, 1768), Zweiter Band, pp. 115-117, footnote by Agricola.
§ According to Spitta in 1736. Bach was in Dresden in 1733 and 1736. Professor C. H. Döring (Zeitsch. für I., Aug., 1898) suggests the first trial may have been in 1733—the second (see next page), 1736.

GRAND PIANOFORTE BY GOTTFRIED SILBERMANN, DRESDEN, ABOUT 1745; NOW IN THE STADTSCHLOSS, POTSDAM.

disapproved of them on account of their weak trebles and heavy touch. We now know, from my examination of the instruments at Potsdam, that he was following Cristofori, and probably had not understood his model or had not attained the skill required to reproduce it. Being annoyed at his failure, he made, or at least showed, no more pianos for some years. Then Agricola mentions a piano made for the Countess of Rudolstadt, and that he submitted another to Bach which met with the great composer's approval. Here follows the often quoted anecdote of Frederick the Great, who, meeting with and approving of pianos made by Silbermann, ordered them for his Royal Palaces. Accounts differ: some say all that Silbermann had made.* According to Forkel the pianofortes of the Freyberg Silbermann pleased the king so much that he set about buying them all, fifteen in number. Mooser,† Silbermann's biographer, says they were in Forkel's time unusable, in different corners of the Royal Palaces. If there were so many as Forkel enumerates, then we must credit Silbermann with an iron determination to persevere in making, for some years previous to Frederick's visit, instruments that would not sell. The king's discernment of the merit of these pianos is not less noteworthy. Three are remaining at the present day, one in each of the Potsdam Palaces associated with Frederick: the Stadtschloss, Sans Souci, and the Neues Palais, in the respective music-rooms, undisturbed as left by him. The instrument in the Neues Palais was described by Burney;‡ I have seen, tried, and examined all three in 1881; a trial rendered possible by privileges graciously accorded to me by the Empress Frederick, then Crown Princess of Prussia. The meeting of old Bach with Frederick the Great brought about by his son, Carl Philipp Emmanuel, took place on April 7, 1747,§ when one at least of these pianos was played upon by Bach—probably the one in the Town Palace here engraved. It would seem that

* Forkel, J. N., "Ueber J. S. Bach's Leben, Kunst und Kunstwerke." Leipzig, 1802.

† Mooser, "Gottfried Silbermann der Orgelbauer" (Langensalza, 1857); also, "Die Zweite Säcular feier des Geburtstages," von Gottfried Silbermann, in the "Zeitschrift für Instrumentenbau," by A. J. Hipkins, 1883, No. 11., Band 3, pp. 119-122.

‡ Burney, Charles, Mus. D., "The present state of music in Germany, the Netherlands, and United Provinces" (London, 1773), Vol. II., p. 144.

§ "Dictionary of Music and Musicians," Art. "Bach" (London, 1879), p. 115.

old Bach never really adopted the pianoforte. It was then a novelty in Germany, and even Carl Philipp Emmanuel Bach, who lived until it was generally accepted everywhere, had little to say for it in his celebrated Essay on the true way to play keyboard instruments.* It is not too much to insist that all J. S. Bach's works composed for the clavichord and harpsichord, no less than those composed for the organ, have to be virtually submitted to transcription, at least in the rendering, when transferred to the pianoforte, and this fact was early recognised, as is shown in Czerny's edition of the Forty-eight Preludes and Fugues. I regard Czerny as a pioneer of the latest school of pianoforte playing which has superseded Clementi and Cramer, and the technical side of Beethoven that had its foundation in the clavichord technique.† Trial of the above-mentioned Czerny edition upon the harpsichord will at once demonstrate the essential difference there is between it and the pianoforte.

The Seven Years' War (1755-62) put an end to Saxon pianoforte making; the country was devastated and the workmen scattered, some finding their way to England, where a fresh start in pianoforte making was made. An old tradition in the workshops has kept these men in remembrance as the "twelve apostles." Hitherto the grand piano, horizontal or upright, had only been made. An upright grand by Christian Ernst Friederici, of Gera, in Saxony, dated 1745, was exhibited in the Royal Albert Hall in 1885‡ by the Brussels Conservatoire, with an interesting example of a simple mechanism resembling that of a Nuremberg clock.§ A similar instrument by the same maker, called by him "Pyramide," has more recently been acquired by Herr Paul de Wit, of Leipzig, for his museum in that city. A suggestion for an upright grand piano

* C. P. E. Bach. "Versuch über die wahre Art das Clavier zu spielen." Berlin, 1753. See Dannreuther, E., "Musical Ornamentation," Part II., p. 3, Novello & Co., London, 1895.

† Consult "A Selection of Studies," by J. B. Cramer, with comments by L. van Beethoven, preface, &c., by J. S. Shedlock (remarks by Anton Schindler). Augener, London, 1893, a publication which throws a strong light upon this fact.

‡ "Guide to the Loan Collection, Inventions Exhibition," A. J. Hipkins (London, 1885, p. 30.

§ A drawing of a Pyramide, also dated 1745, from an old engraving, has been published by Herr de Wit in the "Zeitschrift für Instrumentenbau" (Leipzig), Jahrg. 15, 1 March, 1895. Like Silbermann, Friederici was also an organ builder.

had some years before been made by the French harpsichord maker and inventor, Marius.* To this same Friederici is accredited in Germany the invention of the square piano, about 1758. He is said to have named it Fort Bien, a pun upon Forte Piano.† No square piano by him is forthcoming, but the suggestion came naturally from the clavichord—perhaps from altering a clavichord into a piano, of which frequent examples are to be met with, but showing a very poor and unsatisfactory result. Johann Zumpe, who had been, according to Burney, in Shudi's workshop,‡ had the great merit of introducing the English square piano between 1760-65.§ It was of pleasing form and placed upon a stand. The action, almost rudimentary but efficient, contained what was called the "old man's head," a metal pin with a leather knob on the top to raise the hammer, and the "mopstick" damper raised by a simple jack, which accounts for the name. The dampers (*Sordini*), collectively divided into two halves, bass and treble, were taken off by hand-stops placed within the case of the instrument; another stop brought a long strip of leather, called a "sourdine" (*Sordino*), into contact with the strings to produce a *pizzicato*. The direction for the dampers being raised thus became "senza sordini," and the resumption of their use "con sordini." To use the sourdine or muting stop was "con sordino," to remove it "senza sordino."‖

The compass was five octaves from F to f⁴; in Messrs. Broadwood's specimen, which formerly belonged to Sir George Smart, G to f⁴. This instrument,¶ dated 1763, was obviously experimental,

---

* Rimbault, "History of the Pianoforte," 1860, p. 106. The drawing and description is taken from "Machines et Inventions approuvées par l'Académie Royale des Sciences," Tome Troisième (Paris, 1735). It is claimed for Marius that he submitted the instruments described in this publication to this learned Society as early as the month of February, 1716. As practical inventions their value is very small compared with that of Cristofori.

† In the Fourteenth Annual Report of the Mozarteum at Salzburg, under date of Dec. 19, 1791, we find among the slender possessions of Mozart at the time of his death a "Forte-Biano (*sic*) mit Pedal."

‡ Burney, in the "Cyclopædia or Universal Dictionary of Art, Sciences, and Literature," by Abraham Rees, Vol. XVII., "Harpsichord" (London, 1819).

§ Report of the Great Exhibition, 1851. Fétis says he began his pianoforte studies on a Zumpe Square, dated 1762.

‖ "Dictionary of Music and Musicians." "Sordini" (A. J H.), Vol III., p 637. *Musical Times*, No 630, August 1, 1895, "Beethoven and the Sordino," written by Mr. Shedlock, points out Beethoven's use of "sordini" (plural) and "sordino" (singular) from the MS. indications.

¶ Carl Engel said, very appropriately, Zumpe would never have begun with an experimental keyboard, but with one that was usual.

having seventeen keys in the octave.* Zumpe's success was immediate, and rapidly increasing sale soon brought these pretty instruments into general use. The makers increased also—they were chiefly Germans, and in the last decade of the century there were not less than thirty square piano makers, English and German, sending out their instruments in or from London. The oldest Broadwood square piano known is not dated, but is of this model.† It is in the Morris Steinert Collection, Newhaven, Connecticut, U.S.A.‡ An existing square piano by Sebastian Erard, Paris, 1788, also follows Zumpe in internal construction.

In these instruments the tuning or wrest-pins are, as in the clavichord, inserted along the right hand side of the strings, allowing a considerable length of unused wire between those pins and the belly-bridge, and causing the tuning to be troublesome on account of the stretch required, combined with the difficulty of getting the tension equal owing to the friction on both sides of the belly-bridge. John Broadwood, in 1780, remodelled the case, placing the wrest-plank which carried the tuning-pins along the back. By this change he was enabled to reduce the inordinate length of the unused wire, and also to straighten the keys which had been hitherto left more or less twisted in clavichord fashion. He added a crank damper and patented the new instrument in 1783.§ Broadwood did not, however, get beyond the simple pilot or "old man's head" that lifted the hammer. The merit of introducing in the square piano the "hopper"—a jack with a spring and working in a notch or nose forming the front part of a lever, technically known as the "underhammer"—belongs to John Geib, who in 1786 took out a patent for this improvement,‖ and it was first brought out in the square pianos he made for Messrs. Longman and Broderip, music publishers in Cheapside (a business ultimately merged, through Clementi, into the eminent firm of pianoforte makers, Collard & Collard). When his patent expired the use of the hopper became general. The square piano became gradually

---

* To extend Mesotonic or Mean tone tuning to the keys of E flat and A flat major; with twelve keys, A and B flat major are the limits. Even with seventeen the harmonic minor of F sharp is not endurable.

† Broadwoods have since acquired a John Broadwood square piano, Zumpe model, dated 1774. The earliest date in their books is in 1773, of Broadwood's make.

‡ "The M. Steinert Collection of Keyed and Stringed Instruments," by Morris Steinert, Newhaven, Connecticut (New York. 1893), p. 44.

§ John Broadwood, No. 1,379.   ‖ John Geib, No. 1,571.

enlarged, the sound-board was extended, and in America very large instruments of the kind have been made; it has, however, in England and on the Continent, and even in America, given way before the upright and short grand pianos.

After the Seven Years' War the grand piano was reconstructed on distinct lines, and about the same time in England and Germany—particularly in South Germany. The first piano brought into England had been made by an English monk at Rome, Father Wood, presumably on the model of Cristofori.* It was imported by Mr. Crisp, who appears in Fanny Burney's autobiography, and was afterwards sold by him, according to report, to Mr. Fulke Greville for one hundred guineas. It can hardly have been a successful essay, or it might have become out of order, which was very likely, while there was no one in this country to put it right, inasmuch as only slow movements, such as the Dead March in "Saul," could be played upon it. However, after a few years, the harpsichord maker, Roger Plenius, already mentioned, made one like it. When John Christian Bach arrived in London, in 1759, he appears to have favoured the pianoforte, and, according to Burney in Rees's Cyclopædia, this preference incited the harpsichord makers to try to produce them, but always of the large or grand size; the square piano of Zumpe having had an independent start. I should say neither Shudi nor Kirkman were among these pioneers, but Backers, who was an inventor, although described by Burney as of the second rank, made several, but with no great success. So far as is known, there are none of these early grand pianos existing, and what action was used in them is doubtful: it might have been Cristofori's or a German escapement, to be presently described. Broadwood's books a hundred years ago show the occasional substitution of their new action for the "old movement," a witness to its inferiority. Still, from past experience of old instruments, it is more than likely that in a lumber-room of some historical mansion the "old movement" may still await its discovery. I may mention that I found the only genuine Pipe "Regal"† known to exist anywhere at Blair Castle in Perthshire, in 1868. However, Backers was not content with what he had done; he very soon brought out the so-called English action, which, developed and continued by Stodart and Broadwood, has been the best single escapement action. No

* Burney in "Rees's Cyclopædia," Art. 'Harpsichord.". London, 1819.
† Date, 1630.

piano with it by Backers has been met with, but a name-board of one was existing a few years ago, inscribed " Americus Backers Inventor et Fecit, 1776." * In 1777 Robert Stodart's patent,† in which the designation " grand piano " occurs for the first time, has a correct drawing of this action. Its proportions have been gradually changed as more and more power was sought for. This action has been Broadwood's ; it has the great merit of simplicity combined with durability, and has been found equal to the requirements of Chopin, Henselt, Liszt, Clara Schumann and Hans von Bülow.

Contemporary with Backers' invention in England, or perhaps a little earlier, there appeared that other kind of escapement in South Germany, which, as the Viennese action, enjoyed for years the favour of pianists. Less capable than the English action of producing tone in its varieties, it was easier in respect to execution and brilliant playing generally. In employment it was not restricted to grand pianos, many old German square pianos having been made with a rudimentary form of it, which may have been Friederici's invention, but there is no evidence to directly connect it with him.‡ In its original form the blow is caused by the depression of the key raising the hammer-butt until the back of it comes in contact with a rail at the back of the keyboard, the result being to jerk the hammer to the string. It will be observed in the diagram that the position of the hammer with regard to the key and string is reversed, the hammer-head being inclined towards instead of away from the player. Mozart had played upon such pianos, and in one of his letters to his mother (1777) he describes their tendency to " scheppern " (Austrian dialect, to jar §), in this instance to be translated by " block," a technical term meaning to jam against the strings. Andreas Stein, of Augsburg, improved upon it by adding a hopper escapement and *genouillères*, levers acting as pedals pressed by the knee. There is a grand piano so made by Stein in the Museum of the Brussels Conservatoire, dated 1780, the 0 perhaps doubtful. Unlike the English action, the hopper is a fixture, not rising

---

* " Stainer and Barrett's Dictionary of Musical Terms " (A. J. H.), Novello, 1898, p. 358. " Backers' *Original Forte Piano* " at the Thatched House in St. James's Street, 1771.

† Robert Stodart, Patent No. 1,172.

‡ H. Welcker von Gontershausen, "Der Flügel, oder die Beschaffenheit des Pianos in allen Formen" (Frankfurt-am Main, 1856), p. 57. This writer attributes it to Silbermann, but without evidence.

§ Rimbault, " The Pianoforte," p. 116. The translation here of Mozart's letter needs much correction ; " shiver," for example, is used for " block."

with the key, but attached to the rail behind it. It is the back of the key rising as the front is depressed that causes the escapement and sends the hammer upwards. Stein's daughter, Nannette, who was herself a practical pianoforte maker as well as an accomplished pianist, tuning her piano before she played upon it in public,* was married in 1793 to Andreas Streicher, and under their joint care the Viennese grand piano on this principle reached its highest perfection. Nannette Stein had been a great friend of Beethoven, and his preference for the Stein pianos when at Bonn is known. The Streicher Viennese action shows the last construction of this action: a is the key, b the hopper, i the hopper spring; l is the standard in which the hammer-butt, d, is centred. The set-off button is h, the check f, the damper g.

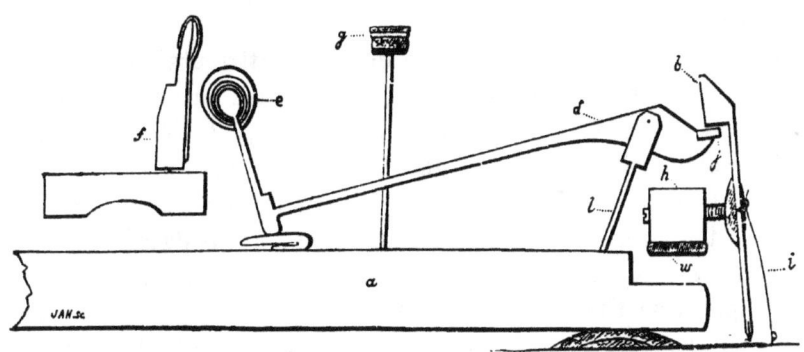

GRAND PIANOFORTE ACTION OF NANNETTE STREICHER, NÉE STEIN, À VIENNA. 1823, AT WINDSOR CASTLE.

The grand piano the Brothers Érard made for Napoleon I., in 1801, has an action on the Stein principle, and is technically as well as historically interesting as showing the point of departure from which Erard started his own action. It has also the row of pedals customary in Austrian and German pianos of the time. Going from left to right the pedals are piano (shifting the action), bassoon (a parchment slip touching the strings for about three octaves), damper; piano "celeste" (muting by thin cloth), and drum and triangle (for Janissary music, the drum-stick striking the underside of the belly of the instrument). A third piano pedal was not uncommon, muting the strings as a sourdine more

* Ernst Pauer, "The Pianist's Dictionary" (Stein), London, 1895.

completely with leather—a suggestion from the late harpsichord.* The contemporary English grand pianos were constant in the use, as now, of two pedals, but the piano pedal by a stop in the block gave the player the choice of two strings or one string, according to the effect sought—the latter being the "una corda" of Beethoven; and the damper pedal, by a divided foot, gave the option of raising the dampers in bass and treble divisions, or, as now, all together. This arrangement of the pedals remained in force until about the year 1830. Complication of the pedals does not apparently coincide in the long run with the pianist's requirements. The piano and damper pedals, the former as a sourdine, were invented by John Broadwood, and patented by him in 1783. The shifting pedal is due to J. Andreas Stein; he called it "Spinetchen," probably because it was "una corda," as in the spinet, one string only to a note.

The first piano made in France has been attributed to Sebastian Erard. It was a square one upon the English principle, and was completed in 1777. We have the authority of Fétis for Erard having made his first grand piano in 1796. He appears to have opened a branch of his business in London, for harps if not for pianofortes, in 1786. His first English patent† is dated 1794, and includes a soft pedal obtained by means of a shifting beam, or rail supporting the hammers, so that they could be removed from three to two strings, and to one. In 1801 came his first patent,‡ in

---

* This arrangement follows the Viennese order of Nannette Streicher, whose full sourdine came No. 5, between the celeste and drum. In the Streicher grand piano at Windsor Castle there are also two knee pedals (*genouillères*), one of which acts upon the drum alone—here a parchment drum-head let into the bottom, and made to sound by means of two pieces of lead. A Viennese grand piano, belonging to Mr. Orchardson, R.A., has eight pedals—viz., (1) Bassoon (bass); (2) shift (una corda); (3) bassoon (lighter); (4) celeste; (5) damper; (6) celeste (duplicate for convenience); (7) drum and bells; (8) bells alone. But the order seems to have varied as well as the number; as according to Adam, "Méthode complète de Piano pour l'enseignement dans les classes du Conservatoire de Musique" (Paris, 1802), we have in the same succession, left to right: (1) Leather (lute or harp); (2) damper; (3) cloth (celeste); (4) shift or una corda (pianissimo); and Steibelt, "Méthode de Piano" (Paris, 1805; Leipzig, 1810): (1) Cloth or "lute"; (2) damper; (3) buff stop (piano or harp); (4) bassoon; (5) pedal, or una corda, here called "celeste" (three strings shifted to one)—the celeste and bassoon stops used in combination with the damper pedal, for an agreeable effect.

† Sebastian Erard, No. 2,016.
‡ *Ibid*, No. 2,502.

which he concerned himself with dynamic changes of tone by touch. In 1808* the idea of the Repetition appears in a modification of the action to afford the power of giving repeated strokes, without missing or failure, by very small motions of the key itself. But this idea was long in attaining fulfilment, and had to wait until 1821† for accomplishment.

The modern upright pianoforte was the invention of an Englishman, John Isaac Hawkins, who is also known as the inventor of the ever-pointed pencil. He was living at the time in Philadelphia, U.S.A., and he patented this instrument there and also in his native country, in 1800. In England the patent was taken out in his father's name, Isaac Hawkins.‡ Prior to his invention there had been upright pianos as there had been upright spinets and harpsichords, but these were the horizontal instruments turned up on the broad end, upon a stand. In his "Portable Grand Pianoforte," as Hawkins called it, the strings descended below the keyboard and the bottom of the instrument was upon the floor, as all upright pianos are now made. Messrs. Broadwood own one of these instruments; § it is remarkable as containing the original essays for many improvements since made use of, or re-invented and developed by modern pianoforte makers. There is a complete iron frame within which the belly is suspended independent of the case; resistance to the drawing power of the strings is also met by metal rods at the back of the case; there is an upper bridge of metal and a system of tuning by mechanical screws; an equal length of string throughout; a hopper action anticipating Wornum's and metal supports for it. So many new ideas were surely never grouped before in one musical instrument. It will now be seen why I have given the rare distinction of originality in invention to Hawkins. Once introduced in this country the rise of the upright piano was rapid. In 1807 the now obsolete but beautiful toned cabinet piano was begun. It was planned by William Southwell,|| but he could only protect by patent a new damper action, Hawkins and Loud having

---

* Sebastian Erard, No. 3,170.
† Pierre Erard, No. 4,631.
‡ Isaac Hawkins, No. 2,446.
§ Engraved in the *English Illustrated Magazine*, Art. "The Pianoforte and its Precursors," A. J. Hipkins (January, 1884), p. 225
|| William Southwell, No. 3,029.

Hipkins—History of the Pianoforte.—Novello.

preceded him; the last-named having, in 1802,* patented a diagonal or oblique high upright piano, in which the historian of the American piano, the late Daniel Spillane,† saw an overstrung piano; there is, unfortunately, no drawing to the patent. A low upright piano was brought out by Wornum with diagonal strings in 1811, and with vertical in 1813. But, notwithstanding Wornum's adherence to the crank lever action adapted by Hawkins, Southwell's hinged sticker action, prefigured in Friederici's upright grand of 1745, and apparently made use of by Loud, was preferred in this country for many years. It had its merits, but the centred action as improved by Wornum is now universally accepted and adopted.

MONUMENT TO BARTOLOMMEO CRISTOFORI, THE INVENTOR OF THE PIANOFORTE.

* Thomas Loud, No. 2,591.
† "History of the American Pianoforte," p. 39. The books, pamphlets, and periodicals referred to in these footnotes form a complete Bibliography of the keyboard stringed instruments.

GLOSSARY OF TERMS.

ACTION.—The mechanical movement of a pianoforte interposed between the keys and the strings.

AGRAFFE.—A brass stud pierced with as many holes as there are strings, to form a note of unisons fixed to the wrest-plank of a piano, and serving as a separate bridge for the particular note. The object of it is to gain an upward bearing for the strings.

ALIQUOT SCALE.—A pianoforte scale which introduces a sympathetic string to certain notes in accordance with the second partial tone, or octave of the note it is to sound with; the half being what is called an aliquot division, measuring without a remainder.

AMPLITUDE.—In acoustics, the full extent of a vibration.

ARCH.—A steel strut, originally of an arched form, fitted between the wrest-plank and the belly-bar of a grand piano and bridging over the cavity up which the hammers rise.

ARCHICEMBALO (*Italian*).—A large harpsichord or cembalo, before which the performer stood to play.

BALANCE.—The poising of a key upon a centre in see-saw fashion to admit of its depression by the finger and consequent movement of the action.

BARS.—Struts of wrought or cast-iron between the wrest-plank and the string-plate adjusted to meet the strain or tension of the strings.

BASSOON PEDAL.—A stop in a pianoforte—the early Viennese or German Fagotzug—that brought a strip of vellum or parchment into contact with the strings to imitate the nasal tone-quality of the wind instrument after which it was named.

BEAM.—The rail holding the hammer-butts or hammer-forks.

BEARING.—The pressure of the strings against or upon a bridge; and plural, bearings, the fourths and fifths that are employed in the tuner's groundwork.

GLOSSARY OF TERMS.

Beats.—Audible pulsations, loudnesses separated by silences; between musical sounds the rate of vibration is not quite the same. The number of them in a given time, say a second, is equal to the difference of the number of vibrations of those tones in the same time. The silences are due to the mutual enfeeblement of the vibrations caused by their not keeping time; the loudnesses to a swelling out when the vibrations concur by which the tone is increased. This maximum intensity is the beat, properly so-called. Beats may be counted mechanically; their presence is easily detected in a piano when octaves or unisons are a little out of tune.

Bebung (*German*).—The *vibrato* possible with a clavichord, but with no other keyboard instrument.

Belly.—The resonance table of wood; the sound or sounding-board in a pianoforte, harpsichord, clavichord, or any stringed instrument.

Belly-bars.—Bars, usually of fir wood, glued to the underside of the belly of a keyboard instrument, and disposed so as to strengthen it against the pressure of the bridge and increase its elasticity in order to facilitate the formation of figures of vibration to respond to and reinforce those communicated through the bridge from the strings.

Bent Side.—The curved or angular side of a pianoforte or harpsichord.

Bourdon Stop.—A sixteen-foot register in a harpsichord, an octave below the normal eight-foot pitch.

Bracings.—Beams of wood or struts of metal disposed to resist the tension or strain of the wire strings.

Breaking Weight.—The strain or tension equivalent to a weight at which a length of wire will break.

Bridge.—In the first place, the conductor of vibration, the substance wood, from the string to the belly of any strung musical instrument. In the second place, the pinned rail upon the wrest-plank, or the metal agraffe or stud with the same object of providing the hither bearing for the string; in a bowed instrument this bearing is called the nut.

British Army Pitch.—The standard B flat tuning-fork at Kneller Hall is 479·3 double vibrations a second at 60° Fahr.; or Equal Temperament C 538. A 452·4.

Buff Stop.—In a harpsichord a slide upon which are fixed small pads of buff leather, which by a hand-stop are brought into contact with one of the unison or equal registers to mute it.

Bundfrei (*German*).—Applied to modern clavichords in which each key has its own strings. To be translated "fret-free," or "unfretted."

Cabinet Piano.—An obsolete upright piano about six feet high.

Capo d'Astro Bar.—A pressure-bar acting as the nearer bearing of the vibrating length of string of a piano—replacing, or supplementary to, the wrest-plank bridge. Capo d'Astro is a corruption of Capo Tasto.

Capo Tasto (*Italian*).—Head fret; the nut of a lute or other similar stringed instrument; also, a false nut screwed through holes in the finger-board and neck, so as to transpose the accordance (*i.e.*, raise the pitch by shortening the strings).

Case.—The outer frame of a keyboard instrument.

Celeste Pedal.—A strip of cloth interposed, by the movement of a pedal for the left foot, between the hammer and the strings; acting as an increase of covering to the hammer and reducing the quantity of tone.

Cembal d'Amour.—A double scaled clavichord with two sound-boards.

Chamber Pitch.—A pitch considered suitable for chamber music.

Check.—The support to the hammer of a piano to obviate its falling too far. Usually of spade form upon a wire stem, the broad part covered with leather and slightly bent back.

Choir or Church Pitch.—A pitch suitable for the Church service.

Cimbalon.—The dulcimer used in a Hungarian Gipsy Band.

Clavecin.—*French* for harpsichord.

Clavichord.—A keyboard instrument like a square piano, the tone produced by tangents instead of hammers.

Clavicitherium.—An upright spinet or harpsichord.

Clavicymbal (*Italian*; Clavicembalo).—A harpsichord or spinet.

Claviorganum.—A spinet or harpsichord with organ registers attached.

Compass.—The full extent of keys of a keyboard.

Core Wire.—The steel wire of a bass string that is overspun with another and finer wire.

Cottage Piano.—An upright piano from four to five feet high.

GLOSSARY OF TERMS.

COVERING WIRE.—The fine copper or other wire that is spun round the steel wire of a bass string, to lessen its rate of vibration.

CYMBAL STOP.—One of the foundation registers of the harpsichord; the longer string of the two unisons in Flemish (and English) harpsichords, available from both keyboards.

DAMPER.—The cloth that by contact stops the vibration of a string, and consequently the sound.

DAMPER LIFTER.—That member of a pianoforte action that raises an over-damper, or draws downward an under-damper.

DAMPER PEDAL.—The right foot pedal, which by raising the dampers throughout leaves the instrument undamped.

DIAPASON NORMAL.—The French Standard pitch since 1859. Fixed at 870 simple, 435 double or complete vibrations for A in the treble clef, at a temperature of 15° Centigrade (59° Fahrenheit).

DRONE.—A pedal note, or note that is intended to sound continuously, as it does in the bagpipe and hurdy gurdy, while other notes are being played.

DULCIMER.—A trapeze-shaped stringed instrument, the sounds of which are produced by hammers held in the player's hands.

DUPLEX SCALE.—Those portions of the wire on either side of the normal vibrating length that are usually left dumb, but are here scaled so as to form aliquot lengths and vibrate in sympathy with the portion that is struck by the hammer.

ENGLISH ACTION.—The direct lever action used in English grand pianos.

EQUAL TEMPERAMENT.—That system of tuning by which all the semitones are of equal width. By this system of tuning ascending fifths and descending fourths are hardly perceptibly flat, but ascending major thirds and sixths are equally much too sharp and minor thirds and sixths too flat.

ESCAPEMENT.—A space that is left between the hammer at its full rise and the strings, necessary for the strings to vibrate and to prevent jarring. A double escapement performs this duty without requiring the key to have returned to rest at its level or equilibrium.

FLÜGEL (*German*).—A grand piano or harpsichord (from the wing shape).

FORTE PEDAL.—*See* Damper Pedal.

FRENCH PITCH.—*See* Diapason Normal.

FRET.—A band round the neck of a lute or viol, pressing or stopping upon which the player gets the particular note produced by that length of string. The term comes from to fret or rub. A clavichord is said to be fretted when more than one note is got from a string.

FUNDAMENTAL.—The first partial tone of a string—that is to say, the string vibrating in its full length in simple pendular vibration between the bridges.

GAMBENWERK (*German*).—A *sostenente* harpsichord with gut strings set in vibration by a wheel precisely as the hurdy gurdy is set in vibration.

GEBUNDEN (*German*).—Applied to those clavichords in which more than one key acted upon the same string or unison strings. To be translated "fretted."

GEIGENWERK (*German*).—*See* Gambenwerk.

GENOUILLÈRE (*French*).—A lever to be pressed by the knee of the player, to act as a pedal.

GIRAFFE.—An upright grand piano raised upon a stand, as formerly made in Germany.

GRAND PIANO.—The long or wing-shaped horizontal pianoforte.

GROUNDWORK.—*See* Bearings.

HAMMER.—The sound exciter of a pianoforte.

HAMMER-BUTT.—The centred butt of the hammer-shank in the so-called English action, shaped with the notch against which the sticker of the hopper works.

HAMMER-FORK.—A fork-shaped base of the stem or shank to the hammer-head, acting upon a centre wire, in a Repetition action.

HAMMER-SHANK.—The shaft or stem of a hammer, fixed by glue in the butt and in the hammer-head, of ordinary actions.

HAMMER-TAIL.—A prolongation of the hammer-head shaped so as to be caught in its descent by the check.

HARMONIC.—The sound proper to an aliquot proportion of a vibrating string produced by touching the string upon the node that characterises it, while using the hammer in the usual way.

HARMONIC BAR.—A pressure bar upon the wrest-plank in the treble part of the scale, intended to increase its rigidity and thereby the purity and clearness of the tone-quality.

HARMONIC SCALE.—The natural scale of partial tones from 1, the whole length of the vibrating string, to $\frac{1}{2}$, the octave; $\frac{1}{3}$, the twelfth; $\frac{1}{4}$, the super-octave or fifteenth; $\frac{1}{5}$, the seventeenth, and so on, in an ever diminishing series.

HARMONIC SEVENTH.—The partial tone of the seventh division of the string—not used in modern harmony on account of its dissonance with the subdominant, supertonic, and other intervals of the accepted scale.

HARPSICHORD.—A jack keyboard instrument with the keyboard at one end and more than one string to a note.

HARP STOP.—A muting register in a harpsichord. *See* Buff Stop.

HEXACHORD.—A diatonic succession of six notes. The Hexachordum Naturale is C, D, E, F, G, A; the Hexachordum Durum, G, A, B natural, C, D, E; and the Hexachordum Molle, F, G, A, B flat, C, D.

HITCH-PIN.—The metal pin upon the string-plate to which the farther or lower end of the string is attached.

HOPPER.—The lever or sticker that raises the hammer and regulates the escapement.

HOPPER SPRING.—The wire spring that regulates the angle of the sticker or hopper, and accelerates its return under the notch or roller.

HURDY GURDY.—A stringed instrument with a lute, or guitar-shaped body, made to sound by the rotation of a wheel.

HYDRAULIC.—Acting by water power.

INFLUENCE.—Strings are said to vibrate by influence when a sound near them, of the same period of vibration, causes them to sound, as by natural law they cannot help doing, sympathetically.

JACK.—The wooden plectrum holder of a spinet or harpsichord.

JUST INTONATION.—Tuning by perfect fifths and thirds, instead of by those intervals tempered.

KEY.—A balanced wooden lever, and also the ivory or ebony covering to the end of it, where the player's fingers touch.

KEYBOARD.—The entire set of keys.

KNELLER HALL PITCH.—*See* British Army pitch.

LAUTENWERK (*German*).—A harpsichord strung with gut instead of wire.

LEVER.—A bar of wood, or it may be metal, used mechanically to overcome a certain resistance by its power derived from the fulcrum or support on which it rests.

Long Measure.—Applied to the lowest octave of a keyboard when the keys descend to the lowest C or F, the last notes in diatonic order.

Loop.—In acoustics the rarefied and extended portion of a wave of vibration.

Lute Stop.—The nearest register of a harpsichord to the player, with its own row of jacks to pluck the strings near to the wrest-plank bearing.

Lyrichord.—1. A wheel and gut-strung harpsichord; 2. A cabinet or high upright pianoforte with a register of plectra plucking the strings at the central or octave node.

Machine Stop.—A composition stop to the left hand of a double (English) harpsichord. By pushing it back and putting down the left pedal, the cymbal or first unison and the octave register are taken off and the lute is put on, leaving the second unison on the lower, and the lute on the upper keyboard only. Releasing the pedal restores the cymbal and octave and takes off the lute.

Mean Tone Temperament.—A tuning by which the major and minor whole tones are replaced by mean whole tones, in the keys with few sharps or flats. The fifths are tuned audibly flat in order that the major thirds in those favoured keys may be just. The chords with more than three sharps or two flats are very dissonant, and the fifth below E flat is called the Wolf from its rapid howling beats.

Mi, Re, Ut.—The three bass notes in descending order E, D, C, denoting the short octave when the lowest apparent key is E. In this arrangement the key G sharp sounds E, that of F sharp D, and E—C.

Monochord.—A sound box with one string, different lengths of which are stopped off by moveable bridges to give notes of different pitch. At one time a popular name for the clavichord.

Mortise.—A hole in wood as in a pianoforte key, pierced by the balance pin. Or to receive a tenon or projecting tongue of wood, to form a joint.

Natural.—A key that is neither a sharp nor a flat, one of the longer level keys, so-called because the scale of C major can be played without touching a sharp or raised key.

NODE.—In acoustics the condensed and consequently narrowed portion of a wave of vibration.

NOTCH.—In the English action the clothed section of the hammer-butt, in which the lever or hopper that gives the blow works.

NUT.—The bearing of a string near the tuning-pegs or pins, also (*le noix*) applied to the roller of a repetition action.

OBLIQUE PIANO.—An upright piano with slanting or diagonal instead of vertical strings.

OCTAVE STOP.—In a harpsichord that register which is an octave higher in pitch than the foundation registers.

ORGANISED SPINET.—A spinet with registers of organ pipes attached. *See* Claviorganum.

ORGANO PIANO.—A piano in which a *sostenente* effect is got by rapid blows set up from small hammers.

OTTAVINA (*Italian*).—A spinet an octave higher than the usual pitch.

OVERSTRUNG.—A disposition of the framing of a piano by which the bass overspun strings are carried over the longer steel strings, instead of being parallel with them.

PARTIAL.—A simple vibrating division of a compound vibrating string.

PEDAL.—A lever to be moved by the foot.

PEDAL MOVEMENT.—The apparatus set in motion by a pedal.

PHILHARMONIC PITCH.—The mean pitch of the London Philharmonic Orchestra, 1846-95; c^2 540 = a^1 454, at 20° C., or 68° F. The Philharmonic Society has since adopted the Diapason Normal as a standard.

PIANETTE.—A very low upright piano, known in Paris as Bébé. The word pianette is of English adaptation, and is of ungrammatical structure, being a masculine noun according to the French language, with a feminine ending.

PIANINO (*Italian*).—A small piano or cottage pianoforte.

PIANO PEDAL.—The left hand pedal reducing the quantity of tone.

PIANO QUATUOR.—A *sostenente* piano intended to reproduce the effect of a violin quartet.

PILOT.—An intermediate wooden or metal upright or prolongation to connect the pianoforte movement or action with the key.

PITCH.—The frequency of vibration of a note is recognised by the ear as a given pitch. The French Standard of 870 simple or 435 complete vibrations in a second for a^1 in the treble clef is now generally accepted, except in England, as the Normal or Standard pitch.

PLECTRUM.—A piece of ivory, horn, wood or metal used in some stringed instruments to elicit their sounds.

PORTAMENTO.—In the clavichord touching notes that are in diatonic or chromatic succession, and a marked pressure to raise the pitch.

PORTATIVE.—A mediæval organ that the player carried, manipulating the bellows and playing at the same time.

POSITIVE.—A mediæval chamber organ that was stationary, usually of two-foot pitch; the player requiring a blower to work the bellows.

PRESSURE BAR.—A metal bar pressing upon the strings of a pianoforte to define their vibrating length at the nearer or wrest-plank end.

PROLONGEMENT (*French*).—*See* Pilot.

PROPER TONE.—Any simple vibrating section belonging to a compound vibrating note. With very slender tubes and wire strings of even diameter the proper tones follow in a regular order and are called harmonic; increase of diameter beyond a certain limit disturbs these vibrational divisions and makes them non-harmonic. As occurs in metal bars, bells, and gongs.

PSALTERY.—A stringed instrument like a dulcimer.

PYRAMID.—An old German appellation for an upright grand piano upon a stand.

PYTHAGOREAN TUNING.—Attributed to Pythagoras, and remaining as the normal system of tuning until the fifteenth century. In this tuning the fifths and fourths are perfect and the major thirds and sixths extremely sharp, the major third a ditone, it being composed of two major whole tones.

RAVALEMENT, MIS EN (*French*).—A lowering, applied to an extension of keyboard compass in the bass, usually to a chromatic filling up, doing away with the " short octave," and carrying the bass down below C.

REGAL.—A sixteenth and seventeenth century beating reed organ, with bellows like a Positive organ. A name occasionally applied to the Portative organ.

REGISTERS.—In a harpsichord the rows of jacks upon slides that are governed by the stops.

REPETITION ACTION.—An action that provides a second escapement after the first has taken place, so that the hammer can strike again before the key has risen to its level or equilibrium.

Repetition Lever.—The upper lever in a repetition grand action, acted upon by the repetition spring.

Repetition Screw.—In a repetition grand action the small screw that controls the rise of the repetition lever when impelled by the spring.

Repetition Spring.—The wire spring that keeps the repetition lever of a double escapement grand action in a raised position, while the sticker or hopper falls back against the roller or notch.

Resonance.—The reinforcement of an original sound.

Resonator.—Any substance that resounds. Applied scientifically to an artifice for separating a partial tone from a compound vibrating note to give it prominence.

Ring Bridge.—In overstrung grand pianos a continuation instead of a separation of the sound-board bridge to carry the bass strings farther back.

Roller.—The rounded projection which receives the blow of the hopper or sticker in the usual repetition grand actions, similar to the " notch " in the English action.

Scale.—A sequence of notes in diatonic order from a keynote to its octave, including all the notes belonging to a particular key, or when including the twelve semitones a " chromatic " scale. The scale of a pianoforte is its full extent of compass from bass to treble. The tuner's scale is the octave from F to f¹ grouped round middle c¹, from which he tunes the rest of the instrument by octaves.

Set Off.—The distance the hammer returns from the string when touched with the most gentle impetus. A workshop name for the escapement.

Sharp.—Technically a raised key, applied to the chromatic notes of the keyboard.

Short Octave or Measure.—The lowest chromatic keys in a keyboard instrument used, as they commonly were in the sixteenth and seventeenth centuries, to complete the Diatonic scale in the bass, thus :—

$$\begin{array}{c} \ D,\ E, \\ C,\ F,\ G,\ A, \end{array} \text{ instead of } \begin{array}{c} \ F\sharp,\ G\sharp, \\ E,\ F,\ G,\ A, \end{array}$$

or—

$$\begin{array}{c} \ A,\ B, \\ G,\ C,\ D,\ E, \end{array} \text{ instead of } \begin{array}{c} \ C\sharp,\ D\sharp, \\ B,\ C,\ D,\ E. \end{array}$$

SLIDES.—The racks in which the harpsichord jacks stand, moved by hand-stops.

SOFT PEDAL.—*See* Piano Pedal.

SORDINI.— Dampers. Before the general use of the right foot pedal it was customary to add *senza sordini* when the hand or knee stop was to be set and the instrument left undamped; *con sordini* implied the release of the stop and return to the normal employment of the dampers.

SOSTENENTE (*Italian*).—Applied to a pianoforte of which the tones are sustained like an harmonium or organ.

SOUND-BOARD OR SOUNDING-BOARD.—*See* Belly.

SOURDINE (*Italian*, Sordino).—A muting contrivance attained by a strip of leather or cloth, brought into contact with the strings by a pedal or *genouillère* to produce a peculiar staccato effect.

SPINET.—A jack keyboard instrument with one string to a note.

SPINET STOP.—An octave stop of a harpsichord.

SPUN STRING.—A wire or other string spun over with a smaller wire or other covering to increase its weight and lessen its rate of vibration.

SQUARE PIANO.—A table-shaped piano.

STICKER.—A small lever or jack of wood used to move the hammer-butt or fork and thus raise the hammer. In the older actions of upright pianos a longer jack glued with a leather hinge to the hammer-butt and raised by the action of the hopper and an intermediate lever.

STOPS.—The handles of the slides working the registers of a harpsichord, resembling the draw-stops of an organ, also the registers themselves.

STRIKING PLACE.—That point of a string against which the hammer impinges to set up vibration.

STRING.—A length of any vibrating material, as wire, gut, or silk.

STRING-PLATE.—The metal plate to which the farther ends of the strings are attached.

STRUT.—A bar of metal having a thrust at each end.

SWELL.—A contrivance in the harpsichord to gain a *crescendo*. In the first instance, by raising a portion of the top or cover of the instrument; later, by a frame of shutters on the principle of a Venetian blind and called the Venetian Swell.

SWISS PINE.—A name applied by pianoforte makers to the finer qualities in growth and grain of *Abies Excelsa*, the Spruce Fir.

SYMPATHETIC VIBRATION.—The vibration of untouched strings by influence of other strings, due to any musical sounds near having the same rate of vibration. *See* Influence.

TANGENT.—A toucher. The name applied to the brass stem that excites the sound of a clavichord.

TAPE.—The tape in the action of an upright piano to accelerate the return of the hammer-butt, and of the hammer itself upon the check.

TENSILE.—Capable of tension.

TENSION.—A property of an elastic string or other substance allowing it to be strained until it is more or less tense.

TETRACHORD.—In Greek music a succession of four notes the extreme of which are the interval of a fourth, in the descending order of two whole tones and a semitone. The inner notes could be tuned down or up: the outer were invariable.

TONE-SUSTAINING PEDAL.—A third pedal allowing the selection of notes to be left undamped, or continuing to vibrate, instead of removing all the dampers, as happens with the usual damper pedal.

TUNING-FORK.—A steel pitch-carrier with two prongs, usually tuned for A or C; for military bands, B flat.

TUNING-HAMMER OR LEVER.—The key with which a keyboard stringed instrument is tuned.

UNA CORDA (*Italian*).—"One string." By the piano pedal the shift of three or two strings to one. No longer used in trichord pianos, but in the time of Beethoven grand pianos had a double shift, from three to two, and again to one string.

UNISON STOP.—Properly the second foundation register in a harpsichord; the shorter of the unison strings in a double keyboard one, and sounding on the lower keyboard only.

UPPER PARTIAL.—Any partial or simple division of a compound vibrating string that is above the first, or Fundamental.

UPRIGHT GRAND PIANO.—Accurately a grand piano placed vertically upon a stand; a kind of instrument obsolete; but applied in the present day to the better kinds of the cottage piano.

VENETIAN SWELL.—*See* Swell.

Vibrato (*Italian*).—A trembling; with the voice, violin, or clavichord the reiteration of a note as a grace, or for expression.

Vibrator.—The initial motor that sets up vibration, in whatever form it may be.

Viennese Action.—The action for grand pianos invented and perfected in Vienna.

Virginal.—A spinet, or generally any jack keyboard instrument.

Wolf.—A bad fifth of very discordant effect in the old mean tone, or any unequal temperament. Usually that at the junction of the sharp and flat keys: G sharp (A flat), (D sharp) E flat.

Wrest.—An old English word; as a verb—to tune; as a noun—a tuning-key.

Wrest-pin.—The pin by which the string attached to it is tuned.

Wrest-plank.—The block of wood, or wood and metal in which the wrest or tuning-pins are inserted.

INDEX OF NAMES.

	PAGE
Adam, J. L.	110
Adlung, Jakob 23, 53, 61,	
62, 65, 86, 87, 94, 96, 102	
Agricola, J. F. 65, 96, 102, 103	
Agricola, Martin	59
Alfonso II. da Este, Duke of Modena	79
Alibert, J. P.	44
Allen, E. Heron	75
Allen, William 15, 16, 17, 18	
Alvise, Giacomo	79
Ambros, A. W. ... 55, 58	
Ammerbach, E. N.	51
Antonio, Infante di Portogallo	99
Aristoxenus 46, 62	
Babcock, Alphæus 15, 17, 18, 19	
Bach, C. P. Emmanuel 61, 64, 103, 104	
Bach, Johann Christian ...	107
Bach, Johann Sebastian, 46, 63, 64, 65, 91, 96, 102, 103, 104	
Backers, Americus ... 107, 108	
Banchieri, Adriano ... 67, 68	
Barnby, Sir Joseph	45
Barre, Sieur de la	93
Bates, Joah	95
Baudet, H. C.	97
Baudin	73
Bayard, The Chevalier ...	68
Bechstein, Carl 14, 22, 24, 31, 35	
Becker, J.	44
Beethoven, L. van 38, 42, 92, 104, 109, 110	
Blaikley, D. J. ... 44, 45	
Blount	69
Blüthner, J. F. ... 22, 24, 33	
Blüthner & Gretschel 33, 35	
Boddington, H.	72

	PAGE
Boehm, Theobald ... 15, 20	
Boesendorfer, L. ... 22, 33	
Bord, Antoine ... 28, 37	
Borso d'Este, Duke	66
Bottée de Toulmon ... 48, 55, 56	
Bridgeland & Jardine ...	20
Brinsmead, John, & Sons ...	44
Broadwood, Henry Fowler ...	17
Broadwood, H. J. Tschudi ...	22
Broadwood, James Shudi 15, 17	
Broadwood, John ... 27, 106, 110	
Broadwood, John, & Sons 12, 14, 16, 18, 22, 29, 31, 32, 35, 36, 80, 90, 105, 107, 111	
Broadwood, W. S.	20
Brown, Mrs. Crosby 70, 75, 100	
Brown & Sharpe	11
Bülow, Hans von	108
Burbure, Léon de ... 70, 94	
Burney, Charles, Mus. Doc. 103, 105, 107	
Burney, Fanny	107
Cadby, Charles	27
Caldera, Luigi	97
Cavaillé-Col. Aristide ...	40
Caxton, William	58
Cersne, Eberhard	55
Chappell & Co.	88
Charles I., King	89
Chatterton, G. J.	64
Chickering, Jonas	19
Chopin, Frédéric ... 38, 41, 108	
Clementi, Muzio ... 92, 104, 106	
Clyffe	66
Cocleus, J.	56
Collard & Collard, 22, 33, 36, 92, 106	
Correr, Count...	75
Costa, Sir Michael	44

INDEX OF NAMES.

	PAGE
Cotter, Rev. Joseph	39
Couchet, Jan 23, 80, 81, 83, 84,	91
Cramer, J. B....	104
Crang	95
Crisp, Samuel	107
Cristofori, Bartolommeo	
31, 99, 100, 101, 102, 103,	
105, 107,	112
Ctesibius	48
Culliford	86, 92
Cummings, W. H.	63
Czerny, Carl	104
Dannreuther, E. ...	51, 104
Day, Capt. C. R.	45
Deschamps, Eustace ...	53
De Wit, Paul	61, 91, 104
Diruta, Girolamo ...	51, 74
Dolmetsch, Arnold	64
Domenico, of Pesaro...	60, 78
Donaldson, George	71
Duarte, G. F. ...	23, 83, 85
Ducange, C. D.	55
Edward VI., King	69
Eitner, Robert ...	49, 56
Elisabeth Farnese, Queen	
(Spain)	102
Elizabeth, Queen ...	66, 69
Elizabeth of York, Queen ...	58
Ellis, A. J., Dr. Sc. 7, 40,	
45, 46, 50, 70, 85,	87
Engel, Carl 49, 52, 64, 69,	
80, 85, 86, 92,	94
Erard, Pierre... ...	17, 35, 111
Erard, Sebastian 19, 35,	
109, 110,	111
Erard, S. & P. 16, 22, 31,	
34, 92, 93,	109
Faber, Daniel	63
Farinelli (Carlo Broschi) ...	102
Ferrini, Giovanni	102
Fétis, F. J. 49, 55, 56, 59, 64,	110
Fischer, P. F.	20

	PAGE
Fleischer, Dr. Oskar	91
Florio	58, 69
Forkel, J. N.	103
Fra Angelico	49
Frederick, H.I.M. Empress...	103
Frederick the Great 72, 99,	103
Friederici, C. E. 104, 105, 108,	112
Fruchador, Fray Raymundo	95
Galilei, Vincenzo	77
Geib, John	106
George III., King	80
Gerbier, Balthazar	89
Gerock...	20
Gerock & Wolf	20
Geronimo, of Bologna ...	78
Gerstenberg, J. D.	62
Gibb, William ...	71, 75
Giustini di Pistoia	99
Goddard, Arabella	108
Godwin, John ...	20, 21
Granville, Mary	97
Gray	97
Greville, Fulke	107
Grove, Sir George ...7, 64, 80,	99
Growvels, Hans	70
Guido d'Arezzo ... 48, 50,	52
Guillaume de Machault ...	54
Hallé, Sir Charles	108
Hamilton, H. Vivian ...	90
Hancock, Crang	23
Handel, G. F. 52, 71, 80,	85
Hänfling, C.	53
Harris, Baker	73
Hauser	48
Haward, Charles ...	71, 72
Hawkins, Isaac	111
Hawkins, John Isaac	
15, 32, 97,	111
Haydn, Hans	95
Hellier, Colonel Shaw ...	44
Helmholtz, H. L. F. von	
7, 30, 39, 40, 45,	70

Hipkins—History of the Pianoforte.—Novello. K

INDEX OF NAMES.

	PAGE
Henry VII., King	59, 66
Henry VIII., King	69, 78, 81, 83
Henselt, Adolphe von	38, 108
Hero of Alexandria	47, 48
Hervé, Samuel	16
Herz, Henri	32, 35
Heywood, John	69
Hicks, Peter	63
Hipkins, Alfred James (A. J. H.)	7, 11, 23, 32, 43, 45, 46, 49, 50, 53, 55, 59, 64, 65, 69, 70, 71, 75, 80, 83, 85, 91, 93, 103, 104, 105, 111
Hitchcock, John	71
Hitchcock, Thomas	71
Hofmann	64
Hogarth, William	73
Hopkins & Rimbault	47, 48
Horsfall	10
Hulmandel	81
Huygens, Constantin	81, 83, 93
Isabella, Queen (Spain)	68, 94, 95
Janko, Paul von	53
Jardine, John	20
John of Aragon, King	54
Jonkbloet	81, 93
Keene, Stephen	71
Kemp	88
Kirckman (Kirkman), Jacob	86, 90, 91, 92, 97, 107
Klinckerfuss, B.	86
Koenig (Poet)	102
Koenig, Rudolf	7
Kraus, Alessandro (Figlio)	60, 61, 78, 100
Krebs, Carl	51, 52, 55, 56, 73, 74, 94
Kriegelstein, J. G.	33
Kütsing, Carl	39
Larchey, Loredan	68
Land, Dr. J. P. N.	81, 83, 85, 93
Leamon, A. G.	72

	PAGE
Lewes, William	78
Leyland, F. R.	87
Lichtenthal, M.	21
Liszt, Franz	38, 41, 108
Longman & Broderip	106
Loud, Thomas	19, 111, 112
Luscinius (Nachtigal)	59
Maffei, Scipione	100, 101, 102
Mahillon, Victor	85, 91
Mahoon	73
Maitland, J. A. Fuller	64
Mantegna	75
Manzoni, Count L.	67
Marco dalle Spinette (dai Cembali)	67
Margaret of Austria	68
Marie Antoinette (Queen)	93
Marius, M.	100, 105
Marot, Clement	68
Martelli, Signora Mocenni	100
Mary Stuart, Queen	69
Mary Tudor, Queen	69
Mason, William	97
Mason & Hamlin	44
Mayer, Daniel	26, 27
Meerens, Charles	89
Merlin, Joseph	95
Mersenne, F. Marin	51, 70
Metzler & Co.	73, 97
Meyer, Conrad	19
Minshen, John	69
Molinet	53
Mooser, Ludwig	103
Mott, Isaac	97
Mozart, W. A.	90, 92, 108
Müller (Martin Miller's Sohn)	10
Murray, Dr. J. A. H.	58, 66
Napoleon I.	109
Newton	47, 48
Nicholas, Sir N. H.	78
Novello & Co.	45

Orcagna 55	Ruckers, Andre (Andries) 80, 85
Orchardson, W. Quiller, R. A. 110	Ruckers, Andre (Andries the younger) 80, 81
Paliarino (Hippolito Cricca, detto) 79	Rudolstadt, Countess of ... 103
Pape, Jean Henri 20	
Paredes, Sancho de 94	Sainsbury, W. N. 89
Pasi, Alessandro 67	Salting, G. 67
Patti, Adelina 45	Samuelson, Sir B. 88
Pauer, Ernst 22, 108, 109	Scaliger, Julius Cæsar 66, 67, 68
Paul, Dr. Oscar ... 99, 102	Scheibler, J. H. 45
Pepys, Samuel 71	Schindler, Anton 104
Philip the Hardy 54	Schlick, Arnold ... 56, 83, 87
Plenius, Roger 90, 96, 97, 107	Schneider, Siegmund ... 65
Pleyel, Ignace 32	Schroeter, Christoph Gottlieb 95, 100
Pleyel, Wolff & Co. 35, 36, 92, 93	
Pöhlmann, Moritz ... 10, 11	Schumann, Clara 108
Pohl, C. F. 90	Schütz, Heinrich 73
Pole, William, Mus. Doc., F.R.S. 11	Selby, Mrs. Luard 94
Ponsicchi, Cesare ... 67, 100, 102	Shakespeare, William ... 73
Prætorius, Michael 50, 51, 56, 57, 70, 74, 75, 85	Shedlock, J. S. ... 104, 105
	Shu li, Burkat (Tschudi, Burkhardt) 72, 90, 91, 92, 95, 105, 107
Puliti, Leto 99, 100	Silbermann, Gottfried 65, 102, 108
Pyne, J. Kendrick 72	Slade 73
Pythagoras 46, 57	Smart, Sir George 105
Rabelais 94	Smith, Bucknall 11
Radino, G. M. 77	Smith, Father 51
Rayleigh, Lord 8	Smith, Hermann 43
Rees, Abraham 105	Smith (Schmidt), John Christopher 80
Reissmann, Dr. August ... 71	
Reynvaan, J. Verscheure 61, 81	Smith, John Christopher (the younger) 80
Riaño, Don Juan 49	
Riehle Bros. 11	Smith, Joseph 15
Rimbault, E. F., LL.D. 47, 48, 49, 59, 64, 67, 69, 100, 108	Snetzler, John 95
	Southgate, T. Lea 63
Ring, F. 86	Southwell, William 32, 111, 112
Rombouts 80	Spence 88
Rose, G. D. 35, 36	Spillane, Daniel 18, 19, 20, 21, 112
Rosso, Annibal 69	Spinetti, Giovanni (Spinetus) 67, 68
Rubens, Sir Peter Paul 81, 89	Spitta, J. A. P. 73
Rubinstein, Anton 38	Steibelt, D. 110
Ruckers, Hans 71, 80, 81, 83, 85	Stein, J. A. ... 108, 109, 110
Ruckers, Jean (Hans, the younger) 80, 84, 85, 86, 87, 89, 90	Stein, Nannette ... 109, 110
	Steinert, Morris 65, 71, 85, 106

INDEX OF NAMES.

	PAGE
Steinway, Henry Engelhard	21
Steinway & Sons 12, 14, 19, 21, 22, 23, 26, 28, 35, 43	
Stivori, Francesco	67
Stodart, Robert	107, 108
Stodart, William	16
Stradivari	90
Street, Joseph	64
Streicher, J. A.	33, 109
Tabel, Hermann	91
Tantini, Sesto	66
Taphouse, T. W.	51
Taskin, Pascal	93
Terme, A.	70
Thalberg, Sigismund	38
Theeuwes, Louis	94
Thibout fils	60
Thom, James	16
Tomkison, Thomas	20
Trasuntino, Alessandro	78
Trasuntino, Vito	80
Tschudi (*see* Shudi).	
Valdrighi, Count L. F.	66, 79
Vander Beest, Martin	71
Vander Straeten, Edmond 53, 54, 58, 68, 81, 82, 88, 94	
Vandyck, Sir A.	81

	PAGE
Van Blankenburg, Quirin 81, 82, 83, 85, 86, 87, 89	
Van de Casteele	77
Van Lerius	80
Van Wilder, Philip	79
Vincentino, Nicoló	80
Virdung, Sebastian 49, 50, 52, 57, 59, 60, 61, 74, 96	
Vitruvius	47, 48
Walker, Adam	97
Warman, J. W.	47
Webster	10
Webster & Horsfall	10
Weckerlin, J. B.	78
Welcker von Gontershausen, H.	108
Westphal, R.	62
Windebank, Sir F.	89
Wolf	20
Wood, Father	107
Woodcroft, Bennett	48
Wornum, Robert 32, 37, 111, 112	
Wyldegrys	59
Wyndham, Charles	73
Young, Thomas	40
Zumpe, Johann	105, 106, 107

Featured Titles from Westphalia Press

Peasant Art in Sweden, Lapland and Iceland
by Charles Holme

This particular work offers a carefully chosen selection of both the decorative and fine arts of Sweden, Iceland, and the northern most region of Finland. A comprehensive survey, it includes paintings, jewelry, textiles, metalwork, carving, furniture and pottery.

The Rise of the Book Plate: An Exemplative of the Art
by W. G. Bowdoin, Introduction by Henry Blackwel

Bookplates were made to denote ownership and hopefully steer the volume back to the rightful shelf if borrowed. They often contained highly stylized writing, drawings, coat of arms, badges or other images of interest to the owner.

The Art of Table Setting, Ancient and Modern
by Claudia Quigley Murphy

The arrangement of a table in terms of cutlery, arrangement, serving style, and timing of courses has changed a great deal over time and now is enjoying renewed interest. The History of the Art of Tablesetting was written by a true expert in the field, Claudia Quigley Murphy.

Understanding Art: Hendrik Willem Van Loon's
How To Look At Pictures by Hendrik Willem Van
Loon, Introduction by Daniel Gutierrez-Sandoval

Hendrik Willem van Loon was a Dutch-American professor, journalist, prolific writer, and illustrator. His most famous work, "The Story of Mankind" earned him the prestigious John Newbery Medal.

The Etchings of Rembrandt: A Study and History
by P. G. Hamerton

Philip Gilbert Hamerton (1834-1894) was an Englishman who was devoted to the arts in numerous forms. Due to the praise, Hamerton stuck with art criticism, and went on to write other works. He also wrote novels, biographies, and reflections on society.

Lankes, His Woodcut Bookplates by Wilbur Macey Stone

Julius John Lankes was born in Buffalo, New York in 1884, and became a prolific woodcut print artist, as well as an author and professor. As a child, he enjoyed working with the scraps of wood his father brought home from the lumber mill where he was employed. Lankes had a lifelong interest in art.

Los Dibujos de Heriberto Juarez / The Drawings of Heriberto Juarez, Edited by Paul Rich

That the drawings here are from life in México is not surprising because Juárez is constantly, and at times impishly, putting art into life and getting art from life. He doesn't think of art as something that is done just in a studio or for that matter kept in museums and looked at on Sundays.

The History of Photography: Carl W. Ackerman's George Eastman by Carl W. Ackerman, Introduction by Daniel Gutierrez-Sandoval

The life of George Eastman is very much a part of the history of contemporary photography. Founder of the Eastman Kodak Company, Eastman was an enthusiastic photographer himself who became instrumental in bringing photography to the mainstream.

Famous Stars of Light Opera by Lewis C. Strang, Introduction by Matthew Brewer

Strang's attempts to quantify the humorous elements of each performer, as well as quotes from the performers themselves attempting to explain their own success, are an interesting exercise in attempting to explain the inexplicable.

The Historic Codfish
by George H. Proctor, Samuel D. Hildreth, William Frank Parsons

There may be 160 representatives in the Massachusetts legislature, but there is only one codfish. The nearly five-foot carving hanging from the ceiling is the third reminder of the importance of fishing to the state. The first was burnt in a 1747 fire and the second destroyed during the Revolution. The present fish was enshrined in 1784.

www.ingramcontent.com/pod-product-compliance
Lightning Source LLC
Chambersburg PA
CBHW061327040426
42444CB00011B/2809